WONDER VERSE

Mystical Musings

First published in Great Britain in 2025 by:

Young Writers
Remus House
Coltsfoot Drive
Peterborough
PE2 9BF
Telephone: 01733 890066
Website: www.youngwriters.co.uk

All Rights Reserved
Book Design by Neila Cepulionyte
© Copyright Contributors 2025
Softback ISBN 978-1-83685-472-2
Printed and bound in the UK by BookPrintingUK
Website: www.bookprintinguk.com
YB0640U

FOREWORD

WELCOME READER,

For Young Writers' latest competition *Wonderverse*, we asked primary school pupils to explore their creativity and write a poem on any topic that inspired them. They rose to the challenge magnificently with some going even further and writing stories too! The result is this fantastic collection of writing in a variety of styles.

Here at Young Writers our aim is to encourage creativity in children and to inspire a love of the written word, so it's great to get such an amazing response, with some absolutely fantastic pieces. This open theme of this competition allowed them to write freely about something they are interested in, which we know helps to engage kids and get them writing. Within these pages you'll find a variety of topics, from hopes, fears and dreams, to favourite things and worlds of imagination. The result is a collection of brilliant writing that showcases the creativity and writing ability of the next generation.

I'd like to congratulate all the young writers in this anthology, I hope this inspires them to continue with their creative writing.

CONTENTS

All Saints' CE Junior School, Warwick

Phoebe Jonathan (9)	1
Oliver Phasey (9)	2
Esmae Parton (9)	3
Olive Aris (8)	4

Blakehill Primary School, Idle

Poppy Russell (10)	5
Isla Regan (10)	6
Isabela Brigg (9)	7
Aaniyah Hussain (9)	8
Evie Sykes (10)	9
Olivia Grace Worrilow (9)	10

Broadfield Primary Academy, Broadfield

Abigail Matilde Silva Geraldes (10)	11
Finley Matthews (9)	12
Somto Eze (9)	13
Samantha Cook-Kensett (9)	14
Tasneem Sekayi (10)	15
Aria-Rose Harris (9)	16
Miruna Voinea (10)	17
Raluca Svet Stoica (10)	18
Liv Kelly (10)	19
Payton Morgan (10)	20
Preston Edwards (9)	21
Bailey Franklin (9)	22

Byker Primary School, Byker

Matthew Atkinson (10)	23
Freddy Pace (10)	24

Divine Odiase Cocuzza (11)	25
Thiago Martinez Rodriguez (10)	26
Bryce Turnbull (10)	27
Amber Andisen (10)	28
Riley Williams (11)	29
Anderle Hepple (10)	30
Parker-James Norton-Lowson (10)	31
Gracie Hodgson (11)	32
Kimberley Ozigbo Esere (11)	33
Oliver Redhead (11)	34
Steven Handyside (10)	35
Miya Patten (11)	36
Connor Shipley (11)	37

Charlton CE Primary School, Dover

Arabella Knight (9)	38

Christ Church CE Primary School, Shieldfield Green

Kendra Erhahaon (9)	39
Rowa Al-Bandag (10)	40
Radin Kefayaty (10)	41
Elizabeth (9)	42
D'Jeina Iamas (9)	43
Poppy Bain (10)	44

East Fulton Primary School, Linwood

Linda Jane Cannon (10)	45

Eyton CIW Voluntary Controlled Primary School, Eyton

Penelope Lambert (9)	46
Albie Eastop-Long (8)	47
Rupert Court (9)	48
Bella Astbury (9)	49
Hallam Aspinall (10)	50
Daisy Davies (8)	51
Nio Eastop-Long (10)	52
Zak Turner (9)	53
Iestyn Hughes (10)	54
Otis (9)	55
Max Owens (8)	56
Ellie Matthews (10)	57
Ruth Alby (9)	58
Leo Owens (10)	59
Laila Cowie-Brazier	60
Lisa Clarke (10)	61
Mabel Cowell (9)	62
Joey Hopkin (9)	63
Erin Williams (8)	64

Greatwood Community Primary And Nursery School, Skipton

Julia Smolarczyk (9)	65
Isla Nicholson (9)	66
Imogen Newman (8)	67
Alyssia Knight (8)	68
Harry Robinson (8)	69
Parker Bailey (8)	70
Elara Houghton (8)	71

Holy Trinity Primary School, Stratford-Upon-Avon

Oliver Kuzma (9)	72
Poppy Hazell (9)	74
Sophia Olivia Haywood (10)	76
Eliza Goldyn (10)	77
Flora Gibbons (10)	78
Autumn Hall (9)	79
Henry Smith (10)	80

Isabelle Williams (10)	81
Milly Simpson (10)	82

John Henry Newman Academy, Littlemore

Eddie Singleton (7)	83
Keturah Prasanth Yerragudla (7)	84
Dougie Singleton (7)	85
Lylah Hawkins (6)	86
Richard Okpala (6)	87
Halona Aimiuwu (6)	88
Beau Morrison (7)	89
Chastity Odo (6)	90
Sophie O'Loughlin (7)	91

Langfaulds Primary School, Glasgow

John McArthur (11)	92
Sophie Gordon (10)	93
Annierose McLucas (10)	94
Islay Ward (11)	95
Juan Antonio (10)	96

Lowbrook Academy, Cox Green

Jayden Yadav (9)	97
Linda Dallarda (8)	98
Kamron Singh Battu (9)	99
Bismun Bhumra (8)	100
Emilia Cripps (9)	101
Eira Dere (9)	102
Henry Gregory (9)	103
Jack Diaz (9)	104
Louis Stevens (9)	105

Loxwood Primary School, Loxwood

Baye Brooker (9)	106
Megan Swann (10)	107
Abigail Ross (10)	108
Amelia McDowell (10)	109
Daisy Roberts (10)	110

Meridian Primary School, Greenwich

Nicola Tedesco (9)	111
Erica Wills (9)	112
Sebastian Lionis	113
Amelia-Rose O'Rourke-Ross (9)	114

Newland St John's CE Academy, Hull

Harry Goodwin (11)	115
Chizaramekpere Ilo (11)	116
Umayr Islam (10)	118
Ted Ntete (11)	119
Saurabh Vishwakarma (10)	120
Korinna Chatizwa (11)	121
Alisia Simionas (11)	122
Charlotte Drake-Davis (11)	123
Jacob Williams (11)	124
Joshua Stevenson (11)	125

Park Academy, Boston

Amelia Arendarska (8)	126
Julian Cichawa (8)	127
Rialivhuwa Thovhakale (9)	128

St Bede's RC Primary School, Darlington

Zoey Udobi (9)	129
Layla Dixon (9)	130
Sophia Winders (9)	132
Charlotte Usher (9)	133
Freddy Knight-Allenby (9)	134
Esme Carr (9)	135

St Cuthbert's Primary School, Glasgow

Manuel Baba Jope Omosu (11)	136
River Warren (11)	137
Tiernan Warren (11)	138
Poppy Johnston (11)	139

Sam Ahmad (11)	140
Declan Atkins (11)	141
Lexi Stewart (11)	142
David Zharov (11)	143

The Gateway Primary Free School, Grays

Lakshmi Surapaneni (10)	144
Grace Ndungu (10)	145
Zoe Ramsey Dsouza (9)	146
Manmeet Jethal (10)	147
Amelia Maule (9)	148
Ornella Zutautaite (9)	149
Al-Hasnaa Mraish (9)	150
Amanda Oreha (9)	151
Elyssa Maule (9)	152

Towie Primary School, Alford

Vaila Ridland (8)	153

Tudor Hall School, Banbury

Olivia Ormazabal (10)	155
Cora Bennett (12)	156
Maisie Gross (12)	158
Mokira Asseez (12)	159
Sofia O (10)	160

Wembrook Primary School, Nuneaton

Misam Limbu (10)	161
Lily-Rose Mason (9)	162
Aysha Ion (10)	167
Phungsama Limbu (7)	168
Liam Bettison (10)	169
Rownak Ahmed (9)	170
Fatima Shakoor Jabeen (11)	171
Sara Lockhat (7)	172
Alex Domin (9)	173
Betsy Scrivens (7)	174
Sharada Hiremath (9)	175
Alivia Green (11)	176

Emilia Kemp (7)	177
Lyra Wilson (8)	178
Kaylen Williams (9)	179
Autumn Wilcox (9)	180
Haleemah Sheikh (9)	181
Esme Crane (9)	182
Liyaanah Sheikh (7)	183
Shianne James (10)	184
Fox Wilcox (9)	185
Jessica King (7)	186
Phoenix Maycock (10)	187
Veron Selmani (10)	215
Demi Adeson (10)	216
Godsglory Medayese (9)	217
Zino Ubu (10)	218

Widey Court Primary School, Crownhill

Hallie Wills (9)	188
River Breckell (10)	189
Adelyn Cox (9)	190
Ella Goodwin (9)	191
Evie S (9)	192
Georgie Sanderson (10)	193
Grace Dalrymple (10)	194
Scarlett Keach (10)	195
Bailey McClure (10)	196

Willow Bank Primary School, Thamesmead

Jamie-Leigh Deverill (10)	197
Tianna Hamilton-Walker (10)	198
Zainab Balougun (10)	200
Aseda Asare (10)	202
Tobi Adetula (11)	203
Love Nwadikeduruibe (11)	204
Kaydie Green Mengot (10)	205
Christabel Jaiyesimi (11)	206
Jayden Mclellen (11)	207
Maris Obi (11)	208
Ethan Turrell (10)	209
Inaaya Mozaddid (10)	210
Jesunifemi Ogunkoya (10)	211
Azizah Balogun (8)	212
Ruby Vuong (9)	213
Millie Ross (10)	214

Four Very Different Times

Winter
Whilst everyone gets colder, we slowly grow older.
Frost freezes spiders' webs, forming nature's masterpieces.
As snow falls, children of all ages rush out the front door in bright red wellies and puffy winter coats.

Spring
Everyone in towns, cities and villages is ready to watch the plants shoot out from beneath the darkness of the soil.
Children sprint outside with their eyes peeled for brightly coloured chocolate eggs, small and large.

Summer
Children rush out of school to pack their bags for beautiful sunsets on the beach and make sandcastles.
As well as being very grumpy on the last day because it's back to school.

Autumn
Leaves of many colours slowly drift from the trees.
Children dress up in scary costumes, asking for sugary treats or candy apples.
Scary carved-out pumpkins with a tiny candle deep inside guard the bright houses.

Phoebe Jonathan (9)
All Saints' CE Junior School, Warwick

A Chocolatey Treat

Snuggled on the sofa,
Like a bird in its nest,
I bite, I crunch, I munch!
I'm excited, I'm happy,
It's delicious, it's sweet,
A really terrific treat.

The sliced banana,
All tasty and soft,
The crumbly biscuits,
Bottom and top.

The delightful ooze,
Dripping down to my feet,
Nutella and banana sandwich,
My favourite treat!

Oliver Phasey (9)
All Saints' CE Junior School, Warwick

School

In Year 4, the days are bright
With lessons learned from morning to night
Math and stories, art to create
Friendships forming, futures so great
Playground laughter, a teacher's smile
Growing and learning, mile by mile
Year 4 is where dreams take flight
A time of wonder and pure delight.

Esmae Parton (9)
All Saints' CE Junior School, Warwick

About Words

I am using five words, see how boring it is.
But, if I use a range of sentences big and small, it sounds better.
I use short sentences for drama,
and long sentences for more information on a subject.
Remember short sentences for drama.
And long, long sentences for more information on the subject.

Olive Aris (8)
All Saints' CE Junior School, Warwick

The Wonders Of Space!

What's up there?
Do we really know?
Come with me, we'll jump in a rocket,
Three, two, one let's go!

Zooming away from our planet,
Watching the world go by,
A strange feeling in my tummy,
Gravity disappears as we soar high.

A cheesy lump in the distance,
Within minutes it is near,
Oh, wait! I know that sight!
It's the moon I've seen appear.

Looking out into the dark,
More planets come to light,
Eight sleeping giants,
Fill me with delight.

Poppy Russell (10)
Blakehill Primary School, Idle

The Space Adventure

S omeone, somewhere is thinking about space
P ippa is that someone
A smart, beautiful girl who enters space
C uriosity is through her mind
E very night she goes to that special place
G ruesome images of aliens freezing on Neptune
"I love it here," she says to herself every time
"R uby, Pippa!" her parents call her and her sister
L ive life like it's a sun-shaped lime.

Isla Regan (10)
Blakehill Primary School, Idle

My Pet Guinea Pigs

Ginger is a ninja
She has pains
But never complains
Her favourite season is autumn
And she isn't a naughty 'un
Her companion is Pickle
And she doesn't half tickle
Pickle is cute
Not like a brute
She is lazy
But not so crazy
She likes greens
Of all scenes
Her favourite month is May
And her favourite thing to do is play!

Isabela Brigg (9)
Blakehill Primary School, Idle

Summertime

Nature's most beautiful time
Of the year is summer,
We see the colourful butterflies flutter.

The flowers are blooming,
The air is fresh and crisp, whilst
The birds are singing.

The leaves are vibrant green,
More than they've ever been.

The sun shines so bright,
I have fun until it's night.

Aaniyah Hussain (9)
Blakehill Primary School, Idle

Big Fish In A Little Dish

I'm Goldie, the goldfish.
My tail goes *swish!*
I live in a dish
And I only have one wish
Which is to get a bigger dish!

Evie Sykes (10)
Blakehill Primary School, Idle

Bestieboos

Roses are red
Violets are blue
I love my
Bestieboo.

Olivia Grace Worrilow (9)
Blakehill Primary School, Idle

Gone But Not Forgotten

We used to laugh until the sun went down,
Now I'm searching for your face in this ghost town,
The memories fade, but the silence stays,
You slipped away like the end of long days.

We thought we'd never change,
But life rearranged,
Now it's just me,
And the ghost of you and me.

You were my home, my safe place to fall,
Now I'm standing here alone with nothing at all,
The echoes of our time still linger in my mind,
But now you're gone... You're gone, and I'm left behind.

I keep holding onto the words unsaid,
The promises we made that are long dead,
The calls we missed, the texts we forgot,
I wish I could rewind and make it stop.

Maybe we'll meet again someday,
When the hurt has healed, when the skies aren't grey
But for now, I'll keep the good times near,
Even if you're no longer here.

Abigail Matilde Silva Geraldes (10)
Broadfield Primary Academy, Broadfield

A Dance Of The Universe

In the vast expanse of the cosmic night,
Where stars and galaxies take flight,
There's a dance that no one sees,
An external waltz of galaxies.

Planets twirl in silent grace,
Moons follow in their embrace,
Comets streak with tails of fire,
A celestial bullet, ever higher.

The sun, a beacon bright and bold,
Tells stories of the ancient android,
Of the stars born in Nebula's womb,
To the quiet tomb of Black Hole's gloom.

Each atom, each particle in play,
Dance to the universe's sway,
A symphony of light and sound
In the silence profound.

So when you gaze up at the sky,
Remember the dance that never dies,
For we are part of this grand ballet,
In the universe's endless dance.

Finley Matthews (9)
Broadfield Primary Academy, Broadfield

Class Confidence

I looked miserable and was miserable,
With new faces staring right at me,
I shuddered at the thought of being ashamed in class,
But seriously, how hard could it be?

I looked at the teacher surreptitiously,
Who was expecting my long-awaited answer,
As I looked to my left around the class,
Suddenly someone caught my eye.

It was a boy looking at me,
He seemed to be giving me a thumbs-up,
And suddenly, I gained my confidence back.

I looked at the teacher,
Who had been standing there with the hope of me getting the answer right,
I finally answered the questions,
I just kept on going,
And then, I heard a round of applause.

Suddenly, school didn't seem so bad,
It just takes a little time.

Somto Eze (9)
Broadfield Primary Academy, Broadfield

Out Of Space

Up on Earth, where no one goes
Not even see the galaxies flow
Where stars meet planets and Mars meet... The new fantasy!
And that's where it all began. The one thousand goddesses!

Earth and sun, sun and Earth
Mars, Jupiter
Moon red and blue
Everything, anything
Not nothing.

So far through a star so fast gives me a push
Whilst it goes past in the blink of an eye
Can barely keep up just to try
Trust me, it's there, out there somewhere
Don't know where, but it's there alright.

I'll reach the stars and bring them to Mars!
I'll be a superstar
Once I reach the star,
Or even Mars...

Samantha Cook-Kensett (9)
Broadfield Primary Academy, Broadfield

Jamaican Culture, Jamaican Pride

Welcome to Jamaica!
Welcome to my pride,
Wait until you see my amazing, colourful vibe.
Markets filled with thick air, floating through the afro hair and making them want to stare at the beautiful shore up ahead.
This is Jamaica! Where joy comes in the morn,
Surrounded by gushing waters, unto the shores - where champions were born.
Jamaica, Jamaica - raise your voice and sing, let your voice and freedom ring.
Just like coconut water, you're good for my heart, and seeing the islands makes me feel a part of the Jamaican culture.
Thanks to Bob Marley and thanks to Usain Bolt, they have brought Jamaica together with their amazing results.

Tasneem Sekayi (10)
Broadfield Primary Academy, Broadfield

The Summer Tree

Not a breeze blows in the summer air
Unblowing leaves of a tree so fair
The chocolate brown bark is as rough as can be
It crumbles, as that's what the eye can see.

Petal-like leaves glint in the midday sun
Light dancing, having fun
The branches keep still, staying put
As the tree sucks water from its roots.

A small bird is bathed in warm light
And compliments that it's rather nice
The little bird snuggles into her nest
In the tree with all the rest.

Aria-Rose Harris (9)
Broadfield Primary Academy, Broadfield

Blast Off!

Ten, nine, eight, seven, six, five, four, three, two, one, blast-off!
We are rising up in rockets, we are streaking around the moon!
We are whizzing through the Milky Way, we hope to get there soon!
We are spinning around in outer space, we are shooting to a star!
We are flashing all our searchlights, we are zooming way past Mars!
We are skimming around a comet, we are tumbling past the sun!
We are landing softly home again!
Crash! Bang! Crash!
Didn't we have fun?!

Miruna Voinea (10)
Broadfield Primary Academy, Broadfield

We Love Earth

The Earth has lived longer than us. The planet is 4.5 billion years old and has had lots of birthdays. Earth is teeming with life, people and animals. We love Earth. It's like a big floating ball in our solar system, like a resting sloth. It swiftly rotates and orbits the sun like a dancing ballerina in the dark sky. The land covers the Earth like a rug or blanket. The water makes it look like it's having a shower. Earth has a friend above called Moon, helping everybody on Earth sleep.

Raluca Svet Stoica (10)
Broadfield Primary Academy, Broadfield

Friendship

F orever by your side,
R eaching out with open hands,
I n laughter, love and light,
E ndless support that understands.
N ever alone, together we stand,
D eep bonds that time can't break,
S haring dreams and moments grand,
H olding tight through every ache.
I n every storm, we find our way,
P romises that never sway,
S weet friendship grows each day.

Liv Kelly (10)
Broadfield Primary Academy, Broadfield

Seasons

S ummer is bright and shiny
E ver did it be rainy and dull?
A t dull days, everyone would be sad, not like in summer!
S un is nice and warm
O riginal days are warm or rainy
N o matter what day it is, do what you want!
S ummer makes people happy, but nothing can make people happier than friends!

Payton Morgan (10)
Broadfield Primary Academy, Broadfield

The Autumn Fall

A mazing gold and amber leaves fall,
U nder the trees, they settle to a crisp surface,
T wirling as they gracefully fall through the cosy breeze,
U nder the red, orange and brown leaves, a spiky creature hides,
M any majestic leaves and creatures lay amongst them,
N ights get longer and days get colder.

Preston Edwards (9)
Broadfield Primary Academy, Broadfield

Winter

W inter wonderland in my mind
 I cicles hanging everywhere outside
 N orth Pole glaciers shift and break
 T rees shiver by frozen lakes
 E very child looks out and shouts, "It's snowing!"
 R oaring fireside, warm and glowing.

Bailey Franklin (9)
Broadfield Primary Academy, Broadfield

War: Fair?

The guerrilla warfare was extreme,
Where was I? Where were they?
The trees shot at us, we shot back.
Bang! Those traps were hidden well.
The ground wasn't safe.
One wrong stop and we were dead.
Crash! We were low on manpower.
Bang! Crash! Boom! I was horrified.

We were told to retreat from the battlefield.
I heard people scream, guns banging, people running.
I shot at them. Even though I couldn't see them.
Bang! The bombs broke down trees.
I started running away, my time was now.
Bang! went the guns, narrowly missing me.

Bang! I was shot in the leg.
I called for a medic, but I was too deep into battle.
I shot at all the trees, not knowing where they were.
The trees spoke Vietnamese, all of them.
I shot at the trees even more than once.
My vision became blurry. It went black.

Matthew Atkinson (10)
Byker Primary School, Byker

What Is A Blingus?

Here you are in a little world,
Or maybe there's more... my mind has just curled!
What if there's more... hidden from us?
What should we call it? How about Blingus?
There's more than meets the eye, or even the mind,
Think about Blingus until it's divine.

Imagine its face, happy or sad,
What is it doing, is it good or bad?
Is Blingus big, small, like a chopstick or a bus?
What fits the name, that creature Blingus?
There's more than meets the eye, or even the mind,
Think about Blingus until it's divine.

Let's go deeper, how about a story,
Maybe it was made in a strange laboratory!
Was it happy, tragic, with drama or fuss?
Think about this creature, think about Blingus!
There's more than meets the eye, or even the mind,
Think about Blingus until it's divine.

Freddy Pace (10)
Byker Primary School, Byker

War Is Terrible

War breaking
I don't know what to do
Everybody is going doolally
Shot after shot, people are dying
I'm not even lying
Hours go by, I am scared to die

All I hear are bullets flying everywhere
Scarcely evading them
Better watch where you step because there could be a landmine anywhere
Cherishing my life because I don't know if I will be able to see my wife again
These could be the last bits of my life
Tell my mom I said goodnight
Hoping I wake up tomorrow alive
Me and my team are going to thrive
And I will stay alive

We are going to thrive!

Divine Odiase Cocuzza (11)
Byker Primary School, Byker

Almighty

When I was a kid, I liked a superhero called All Might. He was a strong hero and the best hero ever. When a villain came to the world, All Might would kill him. *Boom*! He won every fight. One day I was in front of him and started to cry and he said to me that all his life he had been a hero. Then I went to my house and started to think about everything All Might had told me. The next day, I was wondering if I should go to the School of Superheroes.

One year passed, and I was the best hero in the superhero school. Finally, I was gonna be with All Might. Everyone was clapping!

Thiago Martinez Rodriguez (10)
Byker Primary School, Byker

The Galaxies Of Never-Ending Space

Did you know the Earth is 4.6 billion years old, and space is like a piece of sand, trillions of galaxies that have not been explored?

Like the sea, it is littler, and just 10% of the sea has been explored, and space has not even been 0.09% explored.

The moon is the shadow that hit the Earth, killed the dinosaurs, and made them extinct. But it seems what lived in the deep oceans lived.

Not just that, a black hole is millions of light years away, and trillions of times the size of the sun.

Bryce Turnbull (10)
Byker Primary School, Byker

One Sleep Till Christmas

The night before Christmas,
I was lying in bed,
With presents and Santa bunched up in my head.

I was tossing and turning,
I couldn't get to sleep,
When I heard a sound, a tiptoe or a creep.

I opened my eyes,
Then walked down the stairs,
I saw a man in red,
I looked on his chin and saw loads of fluffy hairs.

I ran back to my room,
Then got into bed,
And if I didn't, I would not get presents,
But coal instead.

Amber Andisen (10)
Byker Primary School, Byker

Space Life

I'm up in space
In a superhuman chase,
Flying with no trace,
Do you know your place?

Space is a wonder,
Never know the answer,
Like you will ponder,
Just like Prancer.

Jumping across planets,
Colourful black holes,
Cantering up like Janet,
Jumping like the Super Bowl.

Flying through the stars,
Driving in space cars,
Flying cars, crashing system,
Space is an infinite kingdom.

Riley Williams (11)
Byker Primary School, Byker

Murder In Room Thirteen

What goes on in that room?
What if there are witches flying on brooms?
I always hear *crash, bang, boom!*
What goes on in that room?
The door doesn't open very smooth
When it shuts it goes *crash, bang, boom!*
Room thirteen is not the place to be
When I go past, it makes me not want my tea
The people probably want to break free
One day I walked past room thirteen
Then I heard one big scream.

Anderle Hepple (10)
Byker Primary School, Byker

The Great War

The field is going up in flames
H ard shells of lard in your bones
E veryone put on edge within an instant

G reat streak begins
R eal deaths are shown
E very death makes a life to pass
A soldier going insane
T he war has only just started

W here lives begin they also end
A life is nothing, just an ending
R eal war breaks out.

Parker-James Norton-Lowson (10)
Byker Primary School, Byker

Make-Up, Need To Stop

I've got all the posh stuff,
Do it all day, every week, every year,
Stop now, you need to look for you,
Time goes so fast,
That you need to stop all this for your skin,
Time goes still so fast,
You need to keep your skin clean,
Now you will be so beautiful without it,
Always do what you want,
You need to stop doing bad stuff now,
You've got to quit
Now stop being misbehaved.

Gracie Hodgson (11)
Byker Primary School, Byker

Growing Up

I'm a little girl with a big bulging heart,
I like to dress up and go to the park.
Go to the park, yes, that's what I said,
I love to sit at my princess desk and comb through my hair.

I've grown up now with responsibilities,
Now I feel like I have loads of abilities.
To go to the shop by myself with my friends,
Oh no, I need to keep up with the latest, new trends.

Kimberley Ozigbo Esere (11)
Byker Primary School, Byker

Life

Season go by
Time flies
You're growing up.

You're eight!
Friendships are coming
Your life is growing.

The environment is growing
History is changing
Nature has been defeated by global warming.

People are crying
People are dying
It's just the story of life.

Oliver Redhead (11)
Byker Primary School, Byker

Albert Is My Puppy

Loving him is cute. Before I grow up I would take him. Excited for him to learn. For him to show the world turning. For him to show the world. Albert is a dog. Well, I take him for a walk. He is a Jack Russell and a terrier. He is a little scared but he will get the hang of it.

Steven Handyside (10)
Byker Primary School, Byker

The Moon Gloom

I sat on the moon and played my tune,
I saw the sun, that was fun.
I got in a car and saw a star,
Near a bar,
Travelling in my rocket, I put something in my pocket,
With my locket,
Filling up my bucket,
I heard a rocket coming from a bracket.

Miya Patten (11)
Byker Primary School, Byker

Lost In The Woods

One day two friends went to the forest.
They found a hut in the woods. The lights were on, so they went in. There was nobody in, so they turned the lights off.
But the lights turned back on...
"Help me!"

Connor Shipley (11)
Byker Primary School, Byker

Daddy

Daddy is kind, Daddy is the best,
Daddy is better than all the rest!
He takes me on adventures,
He makes me happy when I'm sad,
I really couldn't wish for a better dad.
I dedicate this poem to him to say, "Thank you,"
For being truly awesome,
I really do love you!

Arabella Knight (9)
Charlton CE Primary School, Dover

Pure Peace

Peace is like a rainbow - so high,
Imagine a beautiful dove high in the sky.
You could always use a little love.

Or pray for a beautiful dove.

If you get knocked down, remember we have love in our hearts.

We are all truly beautiful pieces of art.
If you are in an argument or war, use lots of love.

Never do a nasty shove.

And like I said, peace is like a rainbow - so high,
Imagine a beautiful dove in the sky.
We stand proudly like a pole and shout, "Let us free."
We stamp and shout like raged lions. "We should be free!"

Kendra Erhahaon (9)
Christ Church CE Primary School, Shieldfield Green

Fabulous Friends

Friends are nice,
Friends are kind,
Friends are who you'll never deny.

You might fall out,
Or even fight,
But they will always help you when you cry.

You might have sunny days,
They might have rain,
But friends will help, let me explain why.

Friends are like a bucket of water,
But if you are rude it will fall,
Your friend might start to cry and sigh.

Friends are like fabulous rainbows,
With unique colours and more,
And friends never lie.

Rowa Al-Bandag (10)
Christ Church CE Primary School, Shieldfield Green

Dreams

I'm just sitting in my bed,
Thinking in my head.

Loud thundering outside
Does not stop me from wondering.
I drift away to sleep,
Dreams everywhere.

When I was woken
My mind was open

What are dreams?
It's a mystery to find out
And I might make history.

Unfortunately, I still do not have victory over my dreams.
Maybe they are an illusion,
But I still don't have my solution.

It's a mystery!

Radin Kefayaty (10)
Christ Church CE Primary School, Shieldfield Green

Friendship

Friendship is a thread so fine
Woven through the hands of time
It lifts you when the world feels low
And helps you through the highs and lows

A laugh shared in the darkest night
A whisper in the morning light
No words are needed to understand
The silent strength of a steady hand

Through storms and sun, it will remain
A bond that cannot break or wane
For in the heart where friendship resides
Love and trust forever bide.

Elizabeth (9)
Christ Church CE Primary School, Shieldfield Green

A Field I Stay In And Lie

I hear the birds chirping in trees,
I hear the leaves rustling in the breeze,
I hear the bees as they buzz by,
While in the grassy field I lie.

I see the beautiful butterflies,
I see the new pretty rise,
I see the bird flying high,
While in the grass field I lie.

I smell the grass all green and fresh,
I smell the flowers at their best,
I smell the nearby fields of rye,
While in the grass field I lie.

D'Jeina Iamas (9)
Christ Church CE Primary School, Shieldfield Green

Little Bits Of Stars

Little bits of stars
High up in the sky
Little bits of stars
Beautiful and bright
Count them in the sky
They will blow your mind
Little bits of stars
Say goodbye.

Poppy Bain (10)
Christ Church CE Primary School, Shieldfield Green

Holiday

H ot summer air hitting my skin
O n a sunlounger, loving life!
L ong days and short nights
I don't want to leave
D uring dinner, all the new foods taste amazing!
A t last, deep down you want to go home
Y ay! Finally, I am home!

Linda Jane Cannon (10)
East Fulton Primary School, Linwood

Dogs

Dogs are my favourite kind of pet,
When they are sick, take them to a vet.
Border terriers are the best,
All day they never rest.

They are crazy all day and every day,
I want dogs to be by me all the way.
I love my dogs, they are very sweet,
When they are good they get a treat.

When they go out they are on a lead,
Whenever other dogs come they take the lead.
After the walk, they like to rest,
This poem is to inform you my dogs are the best.

Penelope Lambert (9)
Eyton CIW Voluntary Controlled Primary School, Eyton

Fortnite Career

Started playing two years ago,
I was very slow.
I played on Nintendo Switch,
I tried to post my streams on Twitch.
My favourite skin is Trooper,
He is extremely super.
I will land at Tilted Towers,
Then I drop bomb showers.
I like to use the golden pump
The scope looks like a lump.
I like to win on solo,
I scream, "Marco Polo!"

Albie Eastop-Long (8)
Eyton CIW Voluntary Controlled Primary School, Eyton

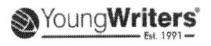

My Bike

On the weekend, I ride my bike,
I know it is one you will like.
My Honda bike is red,
It is heavier than my bed.

I started when I was four,
I really needed a tour.
I fell off once or twice,
It was not very nice.

If you want to ride,
I can be your guide.
I am going to make it pro,
Then I can go, go, go!

Rupert Court (9)
Eyton CIW Voluntary Controlled Primary School, Eyton

The Stupid Old Duck That Was A Nun

Mr Old Duck was getting old in age
He tried to be cool, but people thought he was strange
So, Mr Old Duck decided to become a nun
And finally, he found something fun
And all his life he prayed to God
He always hoped one day not to be in a cof
But as it did come to that section
Mr Old Duck ended up in heaven.
Bye-bye!

Bella Astbury (9)
Eyton CIW Voluntary Controlled Primary School, Eyton

Black History

H eroes of racism, we know today they fought so hard.
I n slavery, they were hit and bullied.
S ometimes they nearly gave up.
T hey are now happy! Really happy, but have sad memories.
O ctober is Black History Month.
R emember everyone who was a slave.
Y ou are lucky to be alive now.

Hallam Aspinall (10)
Eyton CIW Voluntary Controlled Primary School, Eyton

Love For Dragons

D ragons breathe fire
R ain or sun they don't care
A lso, some are mean
G reen or red they could be
O ften sleeping
N ever calm.

L oyalty is in their hands
O ften nice
V ery kind
E verybody is calm.

Daisy Davies (8)
Eyton CIW Voluntary Controlled Primary School, Eyton

Football

F orever I will play football
O ut and in of the field
O thers are jealous of my skills
T ottenham are bottle jobs
B allers have lots of skills
A fter time I will become even better
L eague titles are mine
L iverpool are awful.

Nio Eastop-Long (10)
Eyton CIW Voluntary Controlled Primary School, Eyton

England Football

E ngland is the best national team,
N o one can beat them.
G oals scored every match.
L ook at them dominating the football pitch.
A lexander Arnold is the match favourite.
N o one dominates England.
D efinitely the greatest.

Zak Turner (9)
Eyton CIW Voluntary Controlled Primary School, Eyton

Farming

F avourite animal is a cow
A round the year we must work
R emember the farmers when you eat
M any people love to get muddy
I nside the barn, it is nice and warm
N othing will stop farmers
G ratitude to everyone growing food.

Iestyn Hughes (10)
Eyton CIW Voluntary Controlled Primary School, Eyton

Safety

S afe time on the internet.
A good day in the house on Rocket League.
F eel safe on the internet.
E nding project on Roblox game.
T ry hard, not smart.
Y ou enjoy your time being safe on the internet.

Otis (9)
Eyton CIW Voluntary Controlled Primary School, Eyton

Dragon Poem

D ragons are dangerous.
R ed eyes are like rubies.
A mber skin is like peaches.
G o nowhere near a dragon.
O n the castle where the dragon lives.
N ever go where a dragon lives.

Max Owens (8)
Eyton CIW Voluntary Controlled Primary School, Eyton

Love For Wales

Wales is the best place
It is our kindhearted space
Wales will never die
We will never say bye
Wales is the right place for you
The sky is bright blue
Everyone is as bright as can be
We are all free.

Ellie Matthews (10)
Eyton CIW Voluntary Controlled Primary School, Eyton

Dragon

D ragons breathe fire
R oaring out loud
A s tall as Mount Everest
G ating through the village
O n it goes
N o one is scarier than him.

Ruth Alby (9)
Eyton CIW Voluntary Controlled Primary School, Eyton

The Fire

There was a beautiful fire on the ground,
That everyone gathered around,
It grew, and it grew,
Until everyone knew,
That it had just eaten the playground.

Leo Owens (10)
Eyton CIW Voluntary Controlled Primary School, Eyton

Love

L ove and joy are wonderful
O ver the world is kindness
V aluables are family and friends
E veryone is cool all over the world.

Laila Cowie-Brazier
Eyton CIW Voluntary Controlled Primary School, Eyton

Dragons

D ragons have hard scales
R eally bumpy
A ggressive
G orgeous and beautiful
O ver-reactive
N on-stopping
S o red.

Lisa Clarke (10)
Eyton CIW Voluntary Controlled Primary School, Eyton

Love

L ove and joy are super
O thers make you happy
V alentine's Day means love
E veryone has a perfect match.

Mabel Cowell (9)
Eyton CIW Voluntary Controlled Primary School, Eyton

Wales

W e love Wales
A bout this place
L iving the life
E at fish and chips
S uper Wales.

Joey Hopkin (9)
Eyton CIW Voluntary Controlled Primary School, Eyton

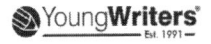

Monkey

Chimp
It likes to run
Climbing, swinging, playing
Eating fruit, nuts and insects
Mammal.

Erin Williams (8)
Eyton CIW Voluntary Controlled Primary School, Eyton

Sloth Cloth Rhyme

Hi, I'm Cloth the Moth!
Come with me to explore my wonderful diet and home.
I eat nectar and fruits.
Yum, yum, scrumpy, yum!
I only come and say bye, hi, 'cause I only come at day and then fly away.
If you have a dog, keep me away from its bog or else I will die, die, die!
Come along, come along my friend to explore my damp, camp house.
Sly ears are before sly abdomen but after my middle segment!
If you catch me, match me to another moth or I'll do it myself!
If you see an echolocating bat, hide me behind a mat. (Quick!)
I'm friends with bugs that live in mugs.

Julia Smolarczyk (9)
Greatwood Community Primary And Nursery School, Skipton

The Police Monkey

P olice monkeys keep trying
O ut they jump at the crime
L ovely at problem-solving
I ndependently on the move
C rime they find all the time
E verything at night.

M oving and growing
O ut of the world, just for a crime
N ow sitting in bed
K eeping rest for the next day
E ach fought all day
Y ep, that's right.

Even on the job, there's a bit of silliness
And on the job, out comes chilliness
Wherever they are
Even in their car
They are police monkeys.

Isla Nicholson (9)
Greatwood Community Primary And Nursery School, Skipton

Clatter, Clatter, What's The Matter?

As I ran to see what was the matter, I saw somebody at the door.
What a clatter it was.
Hobble, bobble.
I walked below the step with a fumble and rumble, as I heard a baby cry.
Hobble, bobble.
Jumped with a clatter, to see what was the matter.
As we walked down the lake - *tumble, rumble, fumble, rumble.*
As I saw a woodlouse at the great tree over there,
Clatter, clatter, what's the matter?

Imogen Newman (8)
Greatwood Community Primary And Nursery School, Skipton

Let Girls Play!

Now, hear me say, let girls play!
It's our dream to be on the team

Running down the wing, left and right
We are always up for the fight

On the pitch, we try our best
We don't give up and never rest

Kicking the ball on the grass
It feels good to make a pass

We make a good team, girl power, we say
One, two, three, let girls play!

Alyssia Knight (8)
Greatwood Community Primary And Nursery School, Skipton

Shelly And Sheldon

In a cosy box where they like to play,
Live Shelly and Sheldon who sleep through the day,
Giant African snails with shells so shiny,
They wiggle and slide, oh, so slimy,
Feeding them lettuce, right there on my hand,
Munching and crunching, they're so grand,
In their cosy little home, they're never alone,
Shelly and Sheldon, in my heart they have grown.

Harry Robinson (8)
Greatwood Community Primary And Nursery School, Skipton

Capybaras And Guinea Pigs

Capybaras, capybaras, what cool creatures
As big as a dog and eat lots of fruit
What fantastic swimmers
Live on the plains, near the lakes
They're cage rodents that chill a lot
Guinea pigs, guinea pigs, as big as a shoe
Like to hide and eat their own poo!
Live in cages and love hay
Who knows what capybaras and guinea pigs get up to?

Parker Bailey (8)
Greatwood Community Primary And Nursery School, Skipton

We Can Do This!

This poem is about
Our tragic mistake.
Throwing rubbish
Is never okay.
If we continue
The creatures will suffer.
What have we done?
What should we do?

We can use recycling bins.
Now that's a good idea!
Turn out the lights
Before it's too late.
We can do this!
We can make it okay!

Elara Houghton (8)
Greatwood Community Primary And Nursery School, Skipton

What Colours Mean

Red is a love colour
With all the flowers and fire
Orange is a tangy colour
With all the juicy oranges.

The extravagant colours amaze me
The wonderful meaning behind them
They show love, hate, friendship and enemies
But colours all stay strong.

Yellow is a sunny colour
With the stars and old cars
Green is the 'go!' colour
With all the grass and happiness.

The extravagant colours amaze me
The wonderful meaning behind them
They show love, hate, friendship and enemies
But colours all stay strong.

Blue is a calm colour
With all the tears and skies
Purple is a party colour
With all the who-knows-what to find.

The extravagant colours amaze me
The wonderful meaning behind them
They show love, hate, friendship and enemies
But colours all stay strong.

Pink is the blossom colour
With the sparkly cherry trees
White is the blank colour
With nothing to see.

The extravagant colours amaze me
The wonderful meaning behind them
They show love, hate, friendship and enemies
But colours all stay strong.

Black is an endless colour
With all staring into space
Rainbows are beautiful colours
That show that everything is meaningful!

The extravagant colours amaze me
The wonderful meaning behind them
They show love, hate, friendship and enemies
But colours all stay strong.

Colours all stay strong.

Oliver Kuzma (9)
Holy Trinity Primary School, Stratford-Upon-Avon

Night Cat

In the pinewood forest at night,
The snowy branches are as prickly as needles,
The bitter, wild berries grow on bushes,
As the moonlight shines on the glittering snow.
You will see shining sap dripping off the trees,
As the patterned snowflakes fall on you,
I look closer into the forest and I see my cat,
I come over and sit with her,
Her eyes glow in the dark,
They twinkle crystal green,
Her razor-sharp teeth are as white as snow,
Her coat is as smooth as leaves in the summer.

With her tight-lipped purr as it calms me,
When she smells those treats she'll come charging at me,
She's as lazy as a sloth.

She hisses like she's a scaly snake,
She'll walk in with a saunter,
I'll pat her on the head with her smooth coat, it calms me,
Her eyes are now reflecting in the night.

I wander back inside,
As I go to bed,
I dream about that wonderful night with my cat.

Poppy Hazell (9)
Holy Trinity Primary School, Stratford-Upon-Avon

A Better Place For Me

Shimmering sunrise in the morning light
Among twisted vibrant vines within the trees
Pointed pink petals on the flowers
Winding trunks and swaying vivid green leaves

Majestic mountains near a crystal clear river
Its crashing calm waterfalls
Diving into a divine new world

Creatures crawl and huddle over dewy earth
Sloths swing branch to branch all day long
Capybaras cuddle and crouch
Jaguars jump afar to reach their prey
With a glisten in their eye as it becomes midday

Citrus smells all around
Fruits are fresh and juicy and slightly sour
Butterflies with rosy, delicate wings
Suck on sickly sweet nectar-like syrup
Birds chirping their love song
Is there a better place for me
It can't get much better.

Sophia Olivia Haywood (10)
Holy Trinity Primary School, Stratford-Upon-Avon

I Love You...?

I never knew you.
You were just another friend.
But when I got to know you,
I let my heart expand.
I couldn't help past memories
That would only make me cry.
I had to forget my love
And give it another try.
So, I fell in love with you
And I will never let you go.
I love you more than anything,
I just had to let you know.
My feelings for you will never change,
Just remember my feelings are true.
I will always pray for you,
I will always go past you,
Even if you're not here,
You will always be in my heart.

Eliza Goldyn (10)
Holy Trinity Primary School, Stratford-Upon-Avon

What's Becoming Of The Forest?

I step into the forest
It's a whole new world
There are pale pink blossoms
To bright red bushes
Tulips and dahlias bursting to open
It's the most beautiful I've seen

The forest floor is covered in vines
I can't help but feel sad to step on it
But I need to see more
I run and run
Deeper and deeper
The forest is changing

Bright colours turn to brown
High trees turn to short
Masses of greenery turn to plain grass fields
What's becoming of the forest?

Flora Gibbons (10)
Holy Trinity Primary School, Stratford-Upon-Avon

Extraordinary Seasons

Autumn is the season of calm
Where wonderful things are being created
And everything changes into greatness.

Winter is the time to have fun
Even when there's no sun
You can build snowmen or even dogs, or cats, or even snowwomen.

Spring is not cold, not warm
Spring is the time for funfairs to happen
And trees to blossom.

Summer is fun
Just fun, fun, fun
You can go swimming and diving and everything.

All the seasons are amazing!

Autumn Hall (9)
Holy Trinity Primary School, Stratford-Upon-Avon

My Dog Lexi

My dog Lexi
She loves many bones
She doesn't like toes
But she also likes chasing cows

My dog Lexi
She loves custard
She doesn't like mustard
But she doesn't want to get busted

My dog Lexi
She loves many tennis balls
She doesn't like busy malls
But one time, she took steak from a stall!

My dog Lexi
She loves birds
She doesn't speak any words
That's my dog Lexi.

Henry Smith (10)
Holy Trinity Primary School, Stratford-Upon-Avon

The Wise Owl That Writes!

When the old oak tree is dark on moonlit nights,
Out of the old oak tree swoops the wise owl that writes:
Glow worms, bees,
Vines and trees,
Moon, fox,
Deer and ox,
Hedgehog, stars,
Jupiter and Mars.

When the old oak tree is dark on moonlit nights,
Back to the old oak tree swoops the wise owl that leaves:
Glow worms, bees,
Vines and trees,
Moon, fox,
Deer and ox,
Hedgehog, stars,
Jupiter and Mars.

Isabelle Williams (10)
Holy Trinity Primary School, Stratford-Upon-Avon

Emotions

Emotions come in different shapes and sizes,
You can be happy or sad,
Strong or brave,
Everyone will have a day.
Love is worry,
Love is weak,
Love makes you warm inside,
Unlike scared, that is something that makes you feel unsafe,
Because there are monsters under your bed.
Joy is like puppies dancing because they are happy and having the time of their lives.
Joy is also like Christmas,
People playing and having fun.

Milly Simpson (10)
Holy Trinity Primary School, Stratford-Upon-Avon

Dinie Dougie

Dinie Dougie travels the sea
Dinie Dougie goes to a disco party

Dinie Dougie goes to space
Dinie Dougie has a friendly face

Dinie Dougie floats around the stars
Dinie Dougie drives race cars

Dinie Dougie reads really cool books
Dinie Dougie is a really good cook

Dinie Dougie is really good at drawing
He creates artwork that is never boring

Dinie Dougie likes to sleep
Dinie Dougie has secrets to keep

Dinie Dougie has letters to send
Dinie Dougie is my best friend.

Eddie Singleton (7)
John Henry Newman Academy, Littlemore

Love The Earth, Keep It Green

Earth needs air crisp and clean,
Always avoid what's mean,
Ride your bike, reduce the smoke,
Trees need tending, thick and oak,
Help the hills hug the sea,
Keep the Earth happy, wild and free.

Love the Earth, love the hills,
Love the air, love the seas,
Love the animals, big and small,
Love the Earth and care for all.

Pick up trash, pick up waste,
Pick up kindness, never haste,
Pick up love, pick up cheer,
Keep the Earth safe and green every year.

Keturah Prasanth Yerragudla (7)
John Henry Newman Academy, Littlemore

Easter The Chick

Easter the chick climbs up a wall
Easter the chick answers a call,
He turns around to sing a song,
But sometimes he gets the words wrong.
Easter the chick is very fluffy,
His feathers are yellow and soft, they are lovely,
Easter the chick can fly when he tries,
But most of the time he is by my side.
Easter the chick eats chocolate cake,
Easter the chick must learn to bake,
He is roly and poly and smiley and kind,
He is the best friend you could ever find.

Dougie Singleton (7)
John Henry Newman Academy, Littlemore

Stripey Loses His Stripes

One gloomy day, in the magic forest, Stripey the tiger lost his stripes. He didn't know where he had left his stripes, so the stripeless tiger started to search for his stripes, but stripe searching was very hungry work. So he went and got his lunch first.

He started to think that finding stripes was boring, so he had a nap and started snoring. He woke up to find he had his stripes back by the morning.

Lylah Hawkins (6)
John Henry Newman Academy, Littlemore

The Mouse

Once, there lived a clever mouse
That lived inside a lonely house.
He wished he had some friendly mice
To play with his newfound dice.
He was so bored playing the dice
So, he decided to make some rice.
He was so bored playing the dice
So, he decided to catch the mice.
The mouse wanted to play with some books
But then he realised there was a stinking boot.

Richard Okpala (6)
John Henry Newman Academy, Littlemore

The Naughty Evil Witch

Once upon a time, there lived a naughty, evil witch and she also decided to hurt all of the animals and cast a dark spell on them.
She turned a rabbit into a toad and a toad into a lioness. She even did the worst spell of all that she could ever do. She made a necklace that was poisoned and gave it to two caged rabbits. She gave a poisoned apple to a tiger and forced the tiger to eat it all.

Halona Aimiuwu (6)
John Henry Newman Academy, Littlemore

The Butterfly

Once upon a time, there were beautiful butterflies in a zoo, but one was an odd one out. All the blue butterflies flew away from the red one. They didn't feel sorry for the red butterfly because they hated that colour. The blues made fun of her and made her feelings sad. But when the zookeeper came, she held out her finger and the red butterfly hopped on and went to the show.

Beau Morrison (7)
John Henry Newman Academy, Littlemore

Oh, What A Wonderful World

The tree shakes and the leaves fall down
The air pushes the flowers
The grass shakes
The butterfly flaps its wings
The children play
Oh, what a wonderful world
The birds sing
The sun goes down
The lion roars
The monkey howls
Our life is beautiful.

Chastity Odo (6)
John Henry Newman Academy, Littlemore

You Can't Give Up

You can't give up school,
You can't give up work,
You can't give up when you are small,
You can't give up when you are big,
You can't give up when you are slow,
You can't give up when you are fast.

Sophie O'Loughlin (7)
John Henry Newman Academy, Littlemore

Hard To Be Me

I was finally born, how cute I was.
My twin had died, how sad it was.

Although it gave me a chance, a chance to be,
Whomever I want, so I was me.

I've done a lot of stupid stuff,
I'm trying my best to be enough.

I'm just not sure if I should be,
What I really want to be.
It's hard to decide.

I just don't know what I seriously want to be,
It's just so hard to be just me.

John McArthur (11)
Langfaulds Primary School, Glasgow

Chico The Dog

Dig in the ground.
Open the door by jumping.
Go on a walk with their owner.

Can't open a door.
Happy all the time.
"I love him."
Chico.
Over the mud.

Got the dog.
Over the fence.
Dog and cat.
Over and under the fence.
Now dig, dog.

She's sorry.
"Oops, dog."
Plays with toys.
Has dinner.
"I love my dog.
Eww, stop peeing!"

Sophie Gordon (10)
Langfaulds Primary School, Glasgow

Summer

S un is shining so bright,
U nited the sun with the sky,
M ake beautiful nights,
M ake warm days,
E veryone is happy,
R ight now everyone is having fun in the summer breeze.

Annierose McLucas (10)
Langfaulds Primary School, Glasgow

Spring Flowers

F lourish.
L ovely flowers
O ver the field
W here I play.
E veryone loves flowers.
R oses smell lovely
S mell nice.

Islay Ward (11)
Langfaulds Primary School, Glasgow

Ronaldo Is The GOAT

Haiku poetry

Ronaldo, the best,
The footballer, Ronaldo.
His son plays football.

He is Portuguese,
In Portugal football team.
Ronaldo is cute.

Juan Antonio (10)
Langfaulds Primary School, Glasgow

The Branch

The thin, chocolate-brown branch sorrowfully sways, waiting for emerald leaves to cover it from the freezing cold,
The fragile wooden arm shivers in the bitter winter cold,
It sways rapidly, knowing its demise,
"Just one more season, then the ruthless cold is gone," the desperate branch murmurs.

The mist reaches across the land like a massive spiderweb,
The fog floats like a ghost haunting the land it meets,
The mystical, mythical army of condensed water spreads like butter,
The ethereal mist lingers, then levitates as the light appears, frightening the dense water vapour.

The snow-covered trees march in union,
The towering oxygen factories loom over tiny creatures,
These titanic buildings make bark reach up to the clouds, as they call to each other,
Nature's monuments stretch like giants and reach the frosty mountains.

Jayden Yadav (9)
Lowbrook Academy, Cox Green

The Branch

The alone branch sways in the faraway mist,
The sharp, pointy sword waiting upon the arrival of spring,
All alone striking figure hangs like a spider's legs,
Delicate and frozen in the cold and misty air,
Nothing around to keep it company.

The magical mist enchants above the glittering horizon,
Whilst swirling majestically in the frozen air,
Pink as a peach, hugging every tree,
It glides across the windswept landscapes.

The wide and dark tissue swaying in the breeze,
The soldiers loomed over the snowy ground leaving its shadows,
It spreads its arms out, pushing some to the side,
Poking the passerby like sharp knives.

Linda Dallarda (8)
Lowbrook Academy, Cox Green

The Branch

Uncontrollably dangling in the air
The deserted branch, patiently waiting for company
Trying to look sturdy but fragile it is
Waiting for the harsh weather to end

Soundlessly it levitates and floats like a ghost
The mist haunts the land, but when the sun comes, it flees to haunt another place
Meander through the air like a ninja undercover
It is a snake violently swallowing the horizon and landscape in a snap

Towering trees looming over, creating shadows
The upright broomsticks sweeping the snow
Animals feel safe when taking shelter
Spiky leaves prodding the air.

Kamron Singh Battu (9)
Lowbrook Academy, Cox Green

The Branch

The enchanting branch, sharp as a knife, is as crooked as a pipe,
It sways and hangs forever with nothing by its side,
Waiting for his demise,
He whispers to everyone in the forest,
And he points to eternity.
The pink, thick, dense mist silently floated to another land,
It gives blossom to the bright blue sky, smiling at people,
It is as dusty as an antique vase,
As it covers countries like an opaque blanket,
The lonely, sorrowful chocolate bar wrapped with green icing,
The tree is a wooden spoon,
Standing tall, the chocolate bar,
Waves in the snowy mountains.

Bismun Bhumra (8)
Lowbrook Academy, Cox Green

The Branch

The beautiful brown branch hanging hopelessly above the nearing ice,
Crooked and abandoned but adapted by snow,
Eye-catching, unable to miss
Bare but magical, one of a kind.

The mist mysteriously meanders into the sunset-pink unknown,
Simply a figure of our imagination.
It glides over towns, welcoming but eerie,
Hovering motionless and out of nowhere springs into action.

Slender metal poles poked into the undergrowth,
Covered in snow and dangling ice,
Crunchy bark, thin but unbreakable,
Extending their arms beyond the clouds.

Emilia Cripps (9)
Lowbrook Academy, Cox Green

The Branch

Looming over the beaming hills,
The brittle branch sways in the glistening sun,
Delicately twisting and turning in the cold wind,
The isolated branch drifts into the unknown.

The hazy mist caged above the ground,
Sways, stuck, nowhere to go,
As damp as water,
Waiting for its victims,
To take them away.

Icy fir trees as cold as ice,
Mist glistening over the landscape,
Like diamonds on a field,
Fir trees are the darkest green,
The fir trees sway silently.

Eira Dere (9)
Lowbrook Academy, Cox Green

The Branch

The mystical branch peers over the mountainside,
The branch sways majestically in the pitch-black sky,
The lanky branch leisurely touches the sandy ground.

The gloomy mist dangles from the sky,
It captures its prey like a slithering snake,
It's a ghost that loves to play,
It haunts you once and then never stops.

As colossal as a giant,
A bristle-covered pool cue,
Like a giant's toothbrush,
It violently vomits on every piece of snow,
Tree, tree, tree.

Henry Gregory (9)
Lowbrook Academy, Cox Green

The Branch

The brown, brittle branch looms out into the valley.
As sharp as a needle,
It hardens in the cold air.
All lonely and isolated,
The branch waits to grow leaves.

The enchanting mist,
It covers the humongous world in a force field.
Can break a sunny day in half,
When the sun comes, it disappears into the unknown.

Trees tower over the ground.
The huge pool cues sway in the wind,
All bare and brown.
They spike anyone walking past.

Jack Diaz (9)
Lowbrook Academy, Cox Green

The Branch

The branch,
The poverty-stricken pretzel stick,
With no one left to play.
With a touch of cocoa,
It glistens on a snowy day.

The mist,
Hangs all day, encasing the trees.
This snowy blanket,
As mysterious as a magic eight-ball.

The fir tree,
A bristle-covered pool cue.
Stabs the air like a dagger,
Vomiting up snow.

Louis Stevens (9)
Lowbrook Academy, Cox Green

Fantastic Gymnastics!

My face will be all smiles if I can perform like Simone Biles,
Flying through the air and tumbling for miles.
I'm going to make it my mission to be the best in the competition,
But for this, I need to work on several different styles.

I need to flip, I hope my feet don't slip.
I need to tumble and I just can't stumble.
I need a perfect roll to achieve my goal.
I need to twist on the ring with such tremendous swing.
I need to jump and bounce and show off my flounce.
I need to spin on the bars but not float off to Mars.

As my hips rotate for a flowing cartwheel, I feel as acrobatic as a performing seal.
I will fly way up high like I'm shooting through the sky with the dream that the show is mine to steal.

Baye Brooker (9)
Loxwood Primary School, Loxwood

You And Me Forever

You and me forever,
You're the light through the dark,
You help me breathe when I can't,
You are my shining star,
You keep me safe from harm,
You're my heart beating fast,
You and me forever,
You support me with your heart,
You come for me when I'm hurt,
You are my positive vibe,
You stop my tears from running,
You help me, I help you,
You and me forever.

Megan Swann (10)
Loxwood Primary School, Loxwood

The Killer Kraken

In the deep, dark sea,
Way, way below where humans can be
Lurks the Kraken, evil as Cronus,
A ghastly nightmare,
Sleeping for years.
Suddenly, it senses a ship
And pushes up off the sea floor.
It surfaces as the vessel passes
And slowly starts to grab the pirates.
Then its tentacles whip,
Then the ship sinks
Into the ocean
And the Kraken resumes its sleep.

Abigail Ross (10)
Loxwood Primary School, Loxwood

Growing Up Hurts

G rowing hurts
R oaring your body like a dragon breathing fire at you
O uch! Stop changing me!
W hat is going on with me?
I hate this
N ow I am all good, living the best life
G rowing hurts, but now it does not hurt so much

U need to love your body
P ush through it.

Amelia McDowell (10)
Loxwood Primary School, Loxwood

Kindness

A smile can make someone's day
A kind word goes a long way
A friendly gesture can mean so much
Spread all the kindness that you hold in your heart
Be smart and don't tear kindness apart
Being kind comes in many ways
Just a quick hello can make someone's day
Just remember, please be kind
And make someone smile.

Daisy Roberts (10)
Loxwood Primary School, Loxwood

Traitors

The dark castle.
The owl flying around.
The dungeon is dead quiet.
Not a single sound is nearby.
Traitors, a mysterious couple,
Come to the castle at night.
Need to be secretive so they don't find out it's them.
But they do get out.
Faithfuls must find out who traitors are but
They usually get out.
Will they do it?
Who knows?
They both do missions and work together.
But traitors talk at night and sometimes in the day.
Traitors talk to faithfuls.
Faithfuls talk to faithfuls...
Finally, Claudia tells us what to do.
Her footsteps around the round table...
Clip, clop, clip, clop...
She talks...
"Who are the traitors?
And who will be banished?"

Nicola Tedesco (9)
Meridian Primary School, Greenwich

Dinosaurs

D inosaurs are big and strong
I guanadons are healthy herbivores
N o dinosaurs live today
O riginally dinosaurs ruled the Earth
S tegosaurus, sharp and spiky
A dinosaur has pointy teeth
U p in the sky, pterodactyls fly
"R oar!" says the tyrannosaur
S cream if you see one!

Erica Wills (9)
Meridian Primary School, Greenwich

Over The Seas

Deep and in the dark abyss, a storm begins to brew
Those above seem to miss the chaos that has ensued

A monster emerges!
The world above oblivious

They swim and swim, but in the dim
They're swallowed, and they're gone!

Sebastian Lionis
Meridian Primary School, Greenwich

Chocolate Cake

C hocolate cake is my fave.
A nd I love it on pink plates.
K isses and hugs come with it too.
E specially if it's your birthday.

Amelia-Rose O'Rourke-Ross (9)
Meridian Primary School, Greenwich

Unique

Y ou are unique no matter what,
O ther people think you are not,
U are like a plant in a pot.

A re you comfy in this certain spot?
R eady for the world outside,
E ager to show your talent wide.

U nique one you are,
N othing can get in your path,
I t is impossible to get away,
Q ueens and kings come in your way,
U need to see what you can be,
E ven if no one can see.

C an you see the world around you?
A re you in capable hands?
R ead your commands,
R ight, you are ready for the world,
Y ou can do this.

O thers believe,
N o one is your obstacle.

Harry Goodwin (11)
Newland St John's CE Academy, Hull

Flames Within Us

Love and hatred, side by side
Two tangled forces, fierce and wide
One lifts you high, the other drags you low
Both burn with fire, yet in different glow.

Love is the sun, warm and bright
A gentle touch, a soft delight
It fills the heart with tender grace
A sweet embrace, a peaceful place.

But hatred is a storm that rages loud
It wraps its fury in a shroud
Cold as ice, sharp as stone
It fills the soul until it's alone.

Love builds bridges, hatred walls
Love whispers, hatred calls
They dance together day by day
In tangled forms, they often play.

Yet love, though bruised, will always rise
A steady flame beneath the skies
For even in the darkest night
It fights to turn the wrong to right.

Love and hatred both exist
In every heart, a tangled twist
But love, though hurt, will always stand
The light that guides the darkest land.

Chizaramekpere Ilo (11)
Newland St John's CE Academy, Hull

A Base In Space!

Space, space: a vast and cosmic place
Where the stars ignite and planets race.
Galaxies swirl, a dizzying sight
A cosmic dance bathed in starlight.

Supernovae explode, a brilliant hue.
Shattering stars, a cosmos anew.
Nebulae bloom where giants once stood
A celestial spectacle, grand and subdued.

Black holes lurk, a gravitational sway
Swallowing stars, night and day.
But life persists in cosmic dust,
A universe in wonders
In which we must
Gaze in awe at the celestial show
Where the cosmos unfolds
And wonders grow.

Space, space. As the stars begin to fade
And cosmic dust forms an array
A silent sigh
Lost in the echoes of the sky.

Umayr Islam (10)
Newland St John's CE Academy, Hull

I Am An Outsider

I'm an outsider at home,
There are several ways to introduce myself,
It's always a guessing game for others,
My features don't give me away,
I am an outsider with my mixed culture,
Ashamed of not being able to speak either language,
I am very conscious about my accent with the different dialects and accents,
I try to imitate it so that I don't sound foreign,
I'm left out of conversations,
They speak English in front of me,
But get tired and switch to their native language,
I pretend to know what they say,
But end up leaving,
I can quickly adapt,
But I'm always in the awkward in-between.

Ted Ntete (11)
Newland St John's CE Academy, Hull

The Biting Snow

The coolness brought the warmth within,
As the frozen fire burnt my skin.
The snow dazed,
And the tinted glass glazed.

Now it feels like I am stuck in a jail,
More like one of those stories in a story tale.
I walk the long drawn-out line,
Followed by the faded footprints of mine.

The biting snow repeated,
As I firmly proceeded.
Wandering around looking for an edge here,
Somewhere at the end of this sphere.

Saw a light at a distance,
A door which felt non-existent.
Opening the door, hoping to succeed,
Questioning myself, where could this lead?

Saurabh Vishwakarma (10)
Newland St John's CE Academy, Hull

The Dawn Of Spring

As the cold of winter begins to fade,
A new season draws in.
A season of life and growing warmth,
March the first, the dawn of spring.

The scent of unspoiled grass,
The aroma of fresh flowers.
The birth of a new lamb, as pure as an angel.
The first steps of a calf, as gentle as the breeze,
March the first, the dawn of spring.

A season of love and joy,
A season of growth and new life.
A new beginning for the world,
A reawakening of the Earth.
March the first, the dawn of spring.

Korinna Chatizwa (11)
Newland St John's CE Academy, Hull

The Little Plant

In the heart of a seed
Buried so deep
A tiny plant
Lay fast asleep

"Wake up," said the sunlight
"Wake up," said the raindrops
So the little plant got up
And shone

He shone all day long
As much as one could seek
In the darkness of the night
The tiny plant went back to dream

The fellow plant was no longer a seedling
Nor was he a mature plant
He burst with beautiful tomatoes
As the sun set on the sky so high
And it made him want to cry.

Alisia Simionas (11)
Newland St John's CE Academy, Hull

Dawn Approaches

The night is quiet, a dark, lamplit street.
A dark, lamplit street with the remains of last night's bitter rain
Sputtered throughout the lonely pavement.
The marvellous moon overlooks the street,
Shimmering in the starry night.
Not a sound to be heard down this dim, dark street.
Dawn approaches, warm, comforting colours of the sunrise.
The street is no longer dark and dim, but rather hopeful.
Dawn approaches, watch in awe of the magical mix of colours that rule the sky.
Look, a new day has begun.

Charlotte Drake-Davis (11)
Newland St John's CE Academy, Hull

Mythical Greece And Its Serpent

In some parts of Greece
A long time ago
Lived an unknown serpent
In its aquatic home

Some say it was magical
Some say it was terrible
Others say it was shocking
But overall, it was impeccable

It was a horror to the bad
Like the stories usually said
But karma doesn't strike
At people who are awake

The serpent was kind
Some people say
But the bad kept ignoring
Causing the creature to decay.

Jacob Williams (11)
Newland St John's CE Academy, Hull

Crazy Video Games

V irtual experience in a crazy world.
I t makes me feel ecstatic.
D o great things
E xplore without limits
O pen your mind

G reat experience
A mazing fun
M ining is a good way to get resources
E nergy: keep it at the max!
S ave or you will lose everything.

Joshua Stevenson (11)
Newland St John's CE Academy, Hull

My Forever Friend

My friend, my companion, my soul,
When I see you, you make me whole,
I long for you so much each day,
And I wish I had more things to say.

My friend, my companion, my heart,
You've been by my side from the start,
With every breath of air I take,
I wish these tears I could fake.

My friend, my companion, my life,
Your farewell as sharp as a knife,
But to know that I will see you again,
Does but relieve this tension and pain.

My friend, my companion, my book,
You've given me so much, but never took,
Now I want to say thank you
For everything you've done and do.

Amelia Arendarska (8)
Park Academy, Boston

The Life Of Mythical Creatures

Dragons fly high in the sky,
While monsters creep up from behind.
Get ready for poetic rhymes,
Because this is about mythical creatures, yet not alive.
A Cyclops feasts on flesh,
And unicorns skip on skies so fresh.
Oh, how nice it would be,
A mythical creature like me.

Julian Cichawa (8)
Park Academy, Boston

Solar System

In our solar system, there are planets that are cold. Mercury, Venus, Jupiter, Saturn, Uranus, and Neptune, make up the solar system.
Sometimes all the planets line up
After 2,000 years.

Rialivhuwa Thovhakale (9)
Park Academy, Boston

The Three-Tailed Fox

In a forest shiny and bright
With the sun that shines its very own light
With all creatures big or small
It's still the fairest of all
If you name them one by one
That's how we have Ton and Ton
That has all creatures just the same size
In a competition with a very big prize
There was an animal that just might have failed
And it was an animal that was three-tailed
Her name was Greta, a pretty name, just right
But sometimes she'd wake up all night
"Ha, ha," said a bird
"Why do you look like a nerd?"
"My best friend is here," said Greta
"This keeps getting better and better."
As the best friend saved Greta
The bird flew away to collect his letter
Greta and her friend were saved
They were even excited because they were getting paid.

Zoey Udobi (9)
St Bede's RC Primary School, Darlington

It's Over

My mind's gone blank, my body is weak,
Could this be my final defeat?

It's not about where I am going, it's what I'm leaving behind,
My beautiful daughter, my wife so kind.

I wish I could tell them how I feel,
As I lay here barely breathing, that's not the deal.

The medicine and doctors are so mighty,
My heart crushing my chest ever so tightly.

My family is all here waiting with me,
I hope to always be there with thee.

I can't speak or move but will make the last moments count,
Even if it's hard as the pressure does mount.

Thinking of beautiful sunsets, the morning sky,
Never again to be seen as my time is nigh.

The humming of the birds and the smell of the flowers,
Wishing I had superpowers.

I hope to say a final goodbye,
But as my soul leaves my body, all I can do is sigh.

It's over.

Layla Dixon (9)
St Bede's RC Primary School, Darlington

I Need Pizza!

I need pizza,
Don't ask why,
I need it now or else I'll die.

I need pizza,
Thin and crispy or deep pan,
Stringy cheese, sweet tomato, I'm its biggest fan.

I need pizza,
Sizzling hot, lukewarm or cold, I don't care,
Large, medium or small, as long as I get a fair share.

I need pizza,
Freshly baked and topped with ham,
Oh, please, oh, please, make it for me, Mam.

I need pizza,
Oven is ticking, it's nearly time,
The pizza will soon be mine.

I need pizza,
Is it ready? The suspense lingers,
Oh no, it is fish fingers!

Sophia Winders (9)
St Bede's RC Primary School, Darlington

Zoe And Poppy

Z oe is a great friend
O bviously, loving and always ready to help
E veryone is jealous of me because I have such a good friend (more than one good friend)

P oppy is great at drama
O nly Shakespeare could top her
P oppy is one of the best friends I have
P oppy never gives up
Y ou could only dream of having such a good friend.

Charlotte Usher (9)
St Bede's RC Primary School, Darlington

Space

Space, a place that is known for black and void,
At its endless space,
We all are sure,
We all just don't want to endure,
This is a poem about space,
Which I really need to ace,
I had a cough,
But soon blast off,
I had a friend called Loyde,
He saw an asteroid,
One, two, three,
We glanced up in glee,
This is my poem,
Written for Golem!

Freddy Knight-Allenby (9)
St Bede's RC Primary School, Darlington

Nature

N ever litter, it affects animals and wildlife
A nd not just affects them, kills them too.
T he thing is we need to help them, but lots of people won't.
U and me can help them by not chopping down trees or doing litter-picking
R ead this and tell more people, please help the environment. From
E sme.

Esme Carr (9)
St Bede's RC Primary School, Darlington

Who Am I?

Who am I?
I am the god of thunder
I always wander with my hammer
And I have armour
My dad is Zeus
He likes fruits
I have a brother named Loki
He is not holy
But he saved me
And now he is in a grave
I have a sister
She destroyed my hammer
But I miss her
I went to Earth and then I got Stormbreaker
And became a record-breaker and a sword-breaker
I am Thor.

Manuel Baba Jope Omosu (11)
St Cuthbert's Primary School, Glasgow

How Time Flies

Sometimes it flies,
Sometimes it crawls,
But it always passes inexorably.
We mark it,
Save it,
Waste it,
Bide it,
Race against it,
We measure it incessantly,
With a passion for precision,
That borders on the obsessive.
We slow down over time.
Everything becomes difficult as it goes.
The end has come and you're gone.
It is *time!*

River Warren (11)
St Cuthbert's Primary School, Glasgow

Summer In A Nutshell

S un glazing down on us from afar,
U nder the scorching hot, bright sun,
M ixing sand and water to make a sand fortress,
M outh watering for freezing cold ice cream,
E very second listening to the water splash back at me,
R emembering every second at the beach and making new memories.

That's summer in a nutshell!

Tiernan Warren (11)
St Cuthbert's Primary School, Glasgow

Summer

S unshine is so bright it hurts my eyes
U mbrellas are stored in the cupboard for a long time
M ango slushes are a must in summertime
M emories are starting to begin, I always have a grin
E veryone wanting a thin chin but will not put the chocolate in the bin
R eady to ride in the summer slide.

Poppy Johnston (11)
St Cuthbert's Primary School, Glasgow

My Robot

My robot is my best friend, you can imagine.
My robot is heroic like Superman.
My robot is as useful as a human.
My robot has two shiny bright spots.
My robot is as cute as a little puppy.
My robot loves the green nature.
My robot loves every single creature.
My robot is the best, it teaches me like a teacher.

Sam Ahmad (11)
St Cuthbert's Primary School, Glasgow

Who Are They?

They are strong
They are known for the Celtic languages
They are thought to have begun with the Hallstatt culture
They are described as wearing brightly coloured clothes
They are known for art and archaeology
They are the Celtic Empire.

Declan Atkins (11)
St Cuthbert's Primary School, Glasgow

Summer

S ummer is the best season ever
U nderneath the blazing sun
M y ice cream melting in the sun
M y tongue licking the ice cream
E verybody laughing and shouting
R unning through the freezing water.

Lexi Stewart (11)
St Cuthbert's Primary School, Glasgow

Autumn

Autumn bottom,
Autumn bottom.
Jackets are a must.
Orange leaves are falling on the ground.
October time is like a rhyme.
It is time for Halloween.

David Zharov (11)
St Cuthbert's Primary School, Glasgow

The Astronaut's Freedom

With a spacesuit so pale, like Snow White's veil,
The airy astronaut jumped out the roaring rocket ship.
The airy astronaut swayed across the milky, rough moon gracefully,
Startled, he halted.
Suddenly, a bright beam of light reflected,
Almost like a truthful and shiny mirror,
Which hit the astronaut's protective visor,
Calm, looking down at the moon's crumbly, gravelly floor,
He realised that at that very moment,
There was freedom from stress and worries,
Bursting it all out,
Twisting, turning, and twirling in glorious space,
Once an astronaut with a spacesuit so stale,
Like Snow White's veil,
Zoomed back to eerie Earth.

Lakshmi Surapaneni (10)
The Gateway Primary Free School, Grays

The Beauty Of Nature

Nature is teeming with life,
Birds singing joyfully in the green, beautiful trees.
Blooming echoes of springtime skies.
Take care of nature, the beauty of the world.

Summer ran away, chased by the cold winter wind.
The green, beautiful trees lost their leaves.
Take care of nature, the beauty of the world.

Spring is here, it is warm again.
Wind, rain and sunshine fills the sky.
Leaves form and it is green again.
Take care of nature, the beauty of the world.

The goodness of nature depends on you.
Take care of nature by planting trees and flowers.
Take care of nature, the beauty of the world.

Grace Ndungu (10)
The Gateway Primary Free School, Grays

Friendship Matters

People are not made to be alone. They need somebody who could be anybody, with whom they can weep with, laugh with, talk with and so much more.
Friendship is loyal. Friendship is teamwork and teamwork is dream work. Be bold, be bright and greet everyone you meet with a smile and a twinkle in your eyes. Slowly but surely, as you do this habit every day, you will see people drawn towards you. A process of thought in their minds will begin to form. They will have a dream desire to have a friend like you, to depend on, to rely on, and to have a person to call a friend.
With six simple words, "Do you want to be friends?" your dream can come true.

Zoe Ramsey Dsouza (9)
The Gateway Primary Free School, Grays

Dance Of The Wildflower Wind

The trees sway side to side,
Gliders gliding in the air with pride.
Monkeys swing from the trees,
Every part of nature has its glees.
As the wind howls and lions roar,
There's always something in nature to adore.
But behind this beautiful view,
There is something that we never knew.
If you go beyond and explore,
You will uncover more
About the mysterious, mystic places
With many traces.
So let your imagination be your guide,
Just so you will find everything that tried to hide.
As you uncover the shocking reality,
You will soon realise you are now free...

Manmeet Jethal (10)
The Gateway Primary Free School, Grays

Nature's Beauty

As the trees sway side to side
The wind gets louder with the butterflies
Monkeys swing vine to vine
The sun shines bright.
Tigers roar up to the clouds
While they swirl beautifully around in the bright sky.
Pandas chew slowly on the thick bamboo
Cockatoos *chirp, chirp, chirp*
Why, they disturb the sleeping bats
And wake up the rats.

When the night comes, the owls awake and hoot
Could it be they spotted a delicious newt?
The forest comes alive
When it gets to dusk
Nature's beauty is a must.

Amelia Maule (9)
The Gateway Primary Free School, Grays

Christmas Dream

As I hear the carols play, leaves stretch and grow
At midnight, the golden stars shine down like shooting stars
As I reach out for the snow, I see that other snowmen have been built
In cold weather seasons, the sky is full of shiny things that sparkle, gleam and glow
These holiday pleasures dazzle us, and yet, deep down, we know
That Christmas has its special gifts
Christmas is for giving and being kind
Shepherds, faith and love
Each gift in its own measure
Was smiled on from above.

Ornella Zutautaite (9)
The Gateway Primary Free School, Grays

Aren't We All Like The Seasons?

Aren't we all like the seasons?
We come and go, come and go
We all have good times and bad times
We all have fun times and boring times
Isn't that so?
We all cook and brew
And the cows moo
Rainclouds or sunshine
It all depends on the day
We can be dark and cold
Or as bright as a summer's day
Autumn or spring
They each take their turn
And winter has its day...
Though shorter than the rest;
In May, we can rest.

Al-Hasnaa Mraish (9)
The Gateway Primary Free School, Grays

Friendship Is A Beauty

Whispers of warmth woven together in wonder.
Laughter's lullaby loyal heart's linked.
Cherished connections, colours of warmth.
Sincere smiles and sounds of serene solidarity.
Harmony in hilarity, the joyful journey of jests.
Fellowship's flames, friendship's fragrant footsteps.
Bond of brightness, a tale of true togetherness.

Amanda Oreha (9)
The Gateway Primary Free School, Grays

The Starry Night Galaxy Sky

The stars at night come out to play
Because in the day they are hidden away.
They sparkle and fly across the sky,
The little children wave as they shoot by.
The planets come out to say hello
Way above the people below.
Venus, Saturn and Mars, along with the stars.

Elyssa Maule (9)
The Gateway Primary Free School, Grays

Don't Mess With These Donkeys

Somebody bullied my donkey friend,
But I knew this had to end.
So I went to see Goat,
But it turned out he wasn't about,
He was on a boat.

So I made a raft.
There was a bit of a draught,
But I did not mind.

I got some glass,
Made a mast,
And at last, it was finished.

So I set off for sea,
Then I found a missing key.
It was for some gold,
That would be rather cold.

So I jumped in,
And I found a tin.
I didn't think much of it but it hit me,
Inside was the gold,

And in front of me was Goat's boat.
So I hopped on.

I was mad but also sad that Goat had left.
But now I was with him he made a deal.
But all I wanted was a meal.

He said, "Give me all your gold."
And I said, "Okay."
And I handed over the cold gold.
We went back to shore.
And Goat let out a baa,
Which made the bullying cows go, "Aah!"
And the bullying stopped.

Vaila Ridland (8)
Towie Primary School, Alford

The Despicable Minions

"What's that yellow creature over there?"
"What do you mean by a yellow creature? There is nothing there."
"Yes, that yellow creature over there."
"Is that what I think it is?"
"What do you think it is?"
"A minion."
"A what?"
"A minion."
"A mignion?"
"No, a minion."
"Wait, there is not only one miglion. There's a whole army of them."
"For goodness sake, it's minion not mignion or miglion. It is minion!"
"Geez, sorry, but did you hear what I said? There is a whole army of mignions."
"Minions!"
"Sorry."

Olivia Ormazabal (10)
Tudor Hall School, Banbury

The Journey

As I travel down the river, all is calm, even the waterfall is peaceful,
Gently coming down to meet its friend, the river,
Who will carry it down to another waterfall and carry on the rhythm of the water.

I see another boat.
We pass silently, so not to disturb the peace.
I gently swerve to avoid a small island.
Slowly, a family of swans pass by me.
A little one tries to break free and follow me but is kept in place.

We all know the law of the river.
We all follow the law of the river.

Every day, from dawn until sunset, you may do as you please on the river,
But sunset comes and all is calm and peaceful.
This is the law of the river.
We all know the law of the river.
We all follow the law of the river.

I swerve the other way.
Oh no, I think,
Here is the law-breaking island.

Everyone follows the law of the river apart from the residents of the law-breaking island.
We have tried and tried again to get it to leave.
We say, "Go to a different river, one where they will let you chuck tomatoes at us."
But no, they stay and annoy us.

Oh well, I will try to pass without bothering them and them bothering the peace of the river.
Yes, we managed it!
The peace of the river is kept.
Spoke too soon, someone less knowledgeable has just been splatted.
Oh well, we all will learn.
One day.
Maybe.

I am reaching the end of my journey.
Tomorrow, I will do it all again as I do it every night.
In the morning, I will have fun and play with everyone,
But for now, I will savour the last minutes of peace.

Cora Bennett (12)
Tudor Hall School, Banbury

Our Wonderverse

The sea is alight with glowing jellyfish,
Come to the surface to shine,
Bright yellow trees can lead you astray,
Perfectly ordered into a line,
The sky can sing with many colours,
It will leave you all in awe,
Canyons tiered in many layers,
I barely notice a single flaw,
The mountains graze the sky,
As I watch them drift on by,
The sea's a turquoise hue,
The perfect shade of blue,
The Great Wall of China still stands strong,
It sings me a beautiful song,
A pristine white cliff stands at the coast,
Now, this place, I love the most.

Maisie Gross (12)
Tudor Hall School, Banbury

Andrew, The Famous Singer

Me and my friend Drew went to Peru,
So as you would do, we got in our canoe.
Wonderverse were coming for you!
I opened my can of canned fruit.
A boy called Stu said, "Can I join you two?"
We said...
"No, we heard you have the flu!"
A door was in our view. C'mon, Drew!
I ran through to this door and it took us to a concert. A concert?
So we danced to a song by Andrew!
I love you, Andrew! I lov-
Wake up, Iona! That's Aunt Sue.

Mokira Asseez (12)
Tudor Hall School, Banbury

Wonderland

Have you ever wondered about Wonderland?
Wonderland?
Yes, Wonderland
What do you mean by Wonderland?
Alice in Wonderland
What Alice and Wonderland?
No, Al...
Have you gone mad?
You don't under...
Oh my God, what are you saying?
I'm saying...
Just spit it out now
I was trying to...
Come on, I don't have all day
Alice in Wonderland!
Oh, why didn't you say earlier?

Sofia O (10)
Tudor Hall School, Banbury

All The Seasons

Starting off, winter, the coldest of all the seasons.
There's always snow coming out of the light blue skies.
It's always cold and chilly.
It's as cold as ice.
Get your hot chocolate ready so you don't get cold.

Next is the prettiest season of all the seasons, spring.
Pretty flowers are always on the green, bright grass.
Beware of the bee, they might sting you.
Pink cherry blossoms on the tree.
Pollen everywhere
Just beware, it's the prettiest season of them all.

Next, the hottest season, which is summer.
Make sure to wear clothes for the summer because it's going to be really hot.
It's always hot.
It's as hot as fire.
Get your ice cream ready, it's going to be hot.

Next is the spookiest season of all the seasons.
Leaves are always red, orange and yellow.
Get your pumpkin ready for Halloween.
Get your costume ready for Halloween.
Get ready for the spookiest season.

Misam Limbu (10)
Wembrook Primary School, Nuneaton

The Trip To Vantopia

Through the magic portal
On the other side...
There's a world called Vantopia
It's a beautiful place
But there's a slight problem
The only way to get there
Is through the haunted house in the Forest of Wonderverse
Find the key, unlock the basement
Open the cupboard, and then walk right through
Oh come on now, don't be afraid
It will be fun!

I'm going to tell you now
What it's like to walk through
I step on the lovely soft pink grass
And stare into the dark blue sky full of stars
A little kid with dark green hair and deep brown eyes came running up to me
Saying, "Hello! Welcome to Vantopia!"
I look all around and hundreds of thousands more jump up
Then I look back

My buddy Jack appeared and screamed, "OMG! It's real!"
The little kid continued, "We are the Zopias."

So what happened, you may ask?
The little kid dragged me to a car
Not any car, but a round car that was floating with blue flashy lights
I hopped in next to the little kid, and she screamed, "Let's get ready to ride!"
The car started to lift up
And like a click... we were in space!
The kid pointed out the window to a massive orange and black gas planet
It was beautiful
My window had the view of a planet called Sapatao
It had a lavender ocean and green land
When we arrived back
A Zopia had made a gift for me!
It was massive!
Bigger than their battleship!

As I very slowly took off the wrapping paper...
It took one hour!
I stepped back and stared at it for at least five seconds until I screamed in joy
You will never believe it...

My own Flyo car! Yes, the cars are called Flyo
I looked at the little kid...
She smiled and ran to her parents, who gave her a big hug
Until their mayor looked at me with a concerned face
He looked at someone...
It was Jack and Max!
Max is one of my best friends, she's hilarious
Jack said with a shaky voice, "Max tried to steal your Flyo!"
I looked at her, she looked down
And dropped a map... So with anger, I shoved her out of the way and...
It was a map of when she got the Flyo, where to attack Vantopia...

So what next...
I stared at the map for a few seconds.
Then I nodded at the army of Vantopia, which was at the portal
They grabbed her and shoved her back into the human world
"Forever was she banished!" said a jokingly deep voice
Not Jack... not the mayor... not anyone I knew from here
But it was someone from Earth...

Someone who looked after me for my entire life
Someone who gave his heart and soul to give me care
It was my... dad!

I ran so fast, the breeze nearly made me fly away
Everyone was a green blob
But I stopped dead in my tracks when I heard the voice of a kid
A little kid...
Until my four-year-old sister came out and hugged me tighter than a happy bear
I hugged my dad after, and we spent most of the day chillin'
While my sister went to play
It was like heaven if I were to ever experience it
The laughter... the joy... the talking... the breeze... it was like home
Best day in Vantopia!
Or was it?

When I got to my Zopo home, I heard the noise I was dreading
Three loud knocks on my door... the pattern was the same as when Max used to come round
I stared through the peephole of the door... and there she was, standing there...
I know the face of when she has an evil plan... that face gives me chills

I was scared so bad, I opened my back door and ran faster than the speed of light
I got to Jack's house and stayed there overnight in his guest bedroom
Until... something out of a nightmare happened
The door fully opened and there stood Max... with the key to my Flyo!
I snatched those keys out of her hand so fast that she fell down
I could tell you now how loud I screamed, Jack came downstairs
He got the army and actually fully banished her

The last day...
Although we had ups and downs
This was the best stay
Bye, Vantopia
I will visit again one day...

Lily-Rose Mason (9)
Wembrook Primary School, Nuneaton

Space Is A Mystery

S taring into the pitch-black void, white paint splattering over the blackness
P lasma is a fourth state of matter that exists in space
A stronomy, a fabulous thing to investigate
C apricorn, a star constellation
E arth, the home planet we live on

I nternational Space Centre, that knows most of space
S atellites, patrolling the planets

A tmosphere, the whole mass of air surrounding the Earth

M ars is the fourth planet from the sun
Y uri Gagarin carried the first human space flight out
S eason, a time of year caused by Earth's tilt
T aurus, another star constellation
E clipse happens when the moon blocks the light from the sun
R adius, an old instrument for measuring the angular distance
Y ear, where we orbit our sun.

Aysha Ion (10)
Wembrook Primary School, Nuneaton

Spring, Easter

S unny days, with air that is lovely and fresh
P ink blossoms from hard trees that fall slowly
R ain is gone now. Fresh air seems like decorations now
I n spring it is finally warm and you can be outside.
N ow, blossoms are beautiful, but decorating them is nice!
G et your eggs ready because you're going to write about Easter!

E aster eggs are very popular, and bonnets are creative.
A n easter gift in Easter will be great! Definitely!
S tunning eggs are good, but playing Easter games is the best.
T ry to find rare eggs in the games!
E aster bonnets are the best and are amazing.
R eady to make, or you can try very well!

Phungsama Limbu (7)
Wembrook Primary School, Nuneaton

Football Journey

Someone called Liam
Started school
He loves football
He was born in England
He was the worst at football but then he started taking lessons
He was slowly getting better
But surprisingly he gained 5-star skills
He is in a team 12 to 14 years old
He was off for a month training then he challenged everyone in the school
He always wins
He was chilling when he got a call from Exeter City
He got signed to academy
But after a couple years, he got a call from Liverpool for first team choice
He scored 890 goals and played 1000 games, he was an icon
He got another call at 36, Man City, but he declined because they're bad
He retired at Liverpool and England.

Liam Bettison (10)
Wembrook Primary School, Nuneaton

Xophorias

X ophorias: A mystical and magical realm,
O utstanding views of tremendous trees and miraculous mountains,
P aradise of peace and beauty,
H uge Xephob plants loom over shrubs, ruler of the undergrowth,
O range and ruby-red skies surround the jasper sun,
R ugs of emerald strips trod on by the majestic creatures of the forest,
I slands of wonder glimmer in the sun's glare, its intensity strong,
A ll you need is the right key to unlock the door,
S ights of strange foreign objects are often said, so *beware* when you enter. Abandon hope for all who enter.

Rownak Ahmed (9)
Wembrook Primary School, Nuneaton

Moonlight's Embrace

Moonlight spills like liquid lace,
Tracing shadows, soft with grace.
A silver breath, a silent call,
Stretching wide, yet touching all.

It slips through the windows, pale and thin,
Brushing dreams that lie within.
It hums in whispers low and deep,
A lullaby the midnight keeps.

Upon the sea, it weaves a thread,
A path where lonely hearts are led.
It paints the hill in ghostly white,
A tender touch, so still, so light.

The world it soothes in quiet beams,
Melting sorrow, mending dreams.
No voice it speaks, yet all can hear,
A hush of light, so soft, so near.

Fatima Shakoor Jabeen (11)
Wembrook Primary School, Nuneaton

Enchanted Forest

Opening the glowing, astonishing door to the enchanted forest, I could already see creatures waiting for me. I thought it was a dream, but no. Why? I don't know! The creatures were beautiful, big and small. All of them were unique in their own special ways. I love the enchanted forest! Some of the creatures I saw were: gorgons! Vampires! Unicorns! A Cyclops! Minotaurs! And Typhons! What would you like to see in the enchanted forest?
Curiously, I wondered what secrets were here. Faintly, I heard footsteps and ran... slowly. I ran back through the door, all the way back home.

Sara Lockhat (7)
Wembrook Primary School, Nuneaton

Lots Of Things

Mental health
It is important
Make sure you stay positive
Less negative.

Spring
Green buds on trees
There are lots of bees
Chasing winter away
Leading spring the way.

Dragon's house
Inside the dragon's house
There is a mouse
The mouse races
Whilst the dragon waits.

Summer
The sun shines bright
It's a really short night
While children play outside
Some others prefer to take a ride.

Alex Domin (9)
Wembrook Primary School, Nuneaton

Fairies Everywhere

All of her magic powers
Can grow lots of flowers.

Her wings begin to flitter
Out comes lots of glitter.
And I as a fairy live in a tree
But lots of other fairies live in the sea.

All of her lovely powers
Can grow lots of flowers.

When I use my magic
It makes people ecstatic.
When I wave my majestic wand
It creates a magic pond.

All of her lovely powers
Can grow lots of flowers!

Betsy Scrivens (7)
Wembrook Primary School, Nuneaton

This Is Me!

My heart is pure as gold,
I am very bold.
This is my shine,
My smile is divine.
I am always happy,
My energy is very zappy.
I love to be very kind,
Beautiful memories in my mind.
My teachers say I'm a nerd,
I like to be heard.
My friends call me crazy,
When I say maths is easy.
My parents call me a 'Google',
I am proud to be a good girl.
I am busy like a bee,
This is me!

Sharada Hiremath (9)
Wembrook Primary School, Nuneaton

Fairies

A morning mist,
A brush of wings,
These are just some fairy things,
The soft stars are shining,
The moon is alight,
The folk of the forest are dancing tonight,
The old house with the long pathway,
The children sleeping away,
A close of a window,
A shut of a door,
The vibrations of the floor,
A goodnight and a kiss on the cheek,
And yet the fairy didn't say a squeak.

Alivia Green (11)
Wembrook Primary School, Nuneaton

The Majestic Unicorn

O', unicorn with your coat so white,
Your beauty is divine,
Dancing and prancing around through nature,
You grow a big smile,
With your coat so white,
It sparkles and shines in the starry night sky,
O', beautiful unicorn I wish you were mine,
Though your magical charm belongs to the precious heart of the depths of the forest,
Where true magic lies.

Emilia Kemp (7)
Wembrook Primary School, Nuneaton

Fantasy Magic

M ajestic fairies
A pricots and berries are nice to share
G alloping across the crystal blue sky. Lots of ducklings start to fly.
I gloos in the coldest bit, that's where penguins like to sit.
C rack, crack, crack goes the egg of a unicorn that's gone back to bed.

Lyra Wilson (8)
Wembrook Primary School, Nuneaton

Welcome To Video Games

Fortnite, Fortnite, Fortnite
Tilted Towers get hit by meteor showers
Flush factory smells, p.u.
Trees, roses and blossoms are where I find you
V-Bucks, I love to spend
On skins, you can't comprehend
I get into a rank unreal
How does that make you feel?

Kaylen Williams (9)
Wembrook Primary School, Nuneaton

Gardening

G ardening is great,
A wesome as well,
R aking and planting,
D on't feed it to your dog,
E xcellent eggplant,
N ot to eat,
I like gardening,
N ever will hate it,
G reat, good, amazing!

Autumn Wilcox (9)
Wembrook Primary School, Nuneaton

I Love Reading

I magination
L iterature
O bservant
V anquish
E nchanted

R omantic
E ngaging
A dventurous
D iverse
I ntriguing
N ever stop reading
G rieving.

Haleemah Sheikh (9)
Wembrook Primary School, Nuneaton

Wembrook

W elcoming to all
E ncouraging others
M aths is good
B reak time of course
R eading and writing
O ff to lunch, we go
O h and don't forget the teachers are the best
K ids have fun at Wembrook.

Esme Crane (9)
Wembrook Primary School, Nuneaton

Nature

N ature, nature
A ll around
T rees, leaves and animals that make a sound
U nder the sea and even on the ground
R abbits burrowing underground, waiting patiently to be found
E verywhere, nature, nature, all around.

Liyaanah Sheikh (7)
Wembrook Primary School, Nuneaton

Space

S erenely drifting, stars in endless chase
P ainting shadows on the canvas of space
A dance of light and time, a cosmic race
C elestial whisper echo, a gentle embrace
E ternal mysteries beckon, a boundless place.

Shianne James (10)
Wembrook Primary School, Nuneaton

Washing

W ashing is boring,
A mazing it's not,
S harks don't live there,
H appy they don't live there,
I n the kitchen sink,
N o! I don't want to do it,
G ardening is better.

Fox Wilcox (9)
Wembrook Primary School, Nuneaton

My Best Friend, Nature

The trees are tall
They touch the sky
Their leaves wave at the birds that fly.

The grass is soft
It tickles my toes.

The sun is warm
It hugs my skin.

Nature's my friend
So wild and free.

Jessica King (7)
Wembrook Primary School, Nuneaton

Hate

H opeful in life
A pplaud others
T ogether we can get it done
E ven though you have been knocked down, get back up.

Phoenix Maycock (10)
Wembrook Primary School, Nuneaton

A Clump Of Moss That Needs A Toss

I'm the clump of moss that needs a toss!
Would you please give me a toss,
Because I'm that piece of moss?

On the ground with nothing to do,
Upside down, trying to get up,
But every time I try, I fail.
One time, someone tried to stick me to a stick
And put me back upside down again.

I look like pieces of mouldy grass,
I'm as green as bottle green.
Most people think I'm not even there,
But I'm a piece of moss.

A piece of moss that needs a toss.

Hallie Wills (9)
Widey Court Primary School, Crownhill

Out Of This World

Get in a rocket,
Fly up high,
Oh gosh, oh my...
The peak of dawn, down below,
The moon is shining to and fro.

The sun, oh so bright,
It's blinding me,
Oh, what a sight.
The moonwalkers research and explore,
A whole new world outside their door.

And here is what I've come to see,
A planet parade,
It astounds me.
Now we've had our fun,
A journey back to Earth,
Soaring past the setting sun.

River Breckell (10)
Widey Court Primary School, Crownhill

The Christmas Journey

Elves come together,
Through fields of litter and woods,
Be careful on the slippery moss and sticky-up branches.
When you fall you fall with a *bang!* and a *crash!* and a *bang!*
Through meadows of green and yellowy sand,
You may come across the boss,
His name is Flause and he is the brother of Santa Claus,
But the elves come together to make a team,
To fight for the rights of our class team.

Adelyn Cox (9)
Widey Court Primary School, Crownhill

Don't

Don't!
Don't do, don't do, don't do that
Don't pull faces, don't tease the cat
Don't put Dan in a can
Don't put a key in the tea
Don't put a bear in the chair
Don't go to jail, eat kale
Don't read a poem or kiss Owen
Don't be a cherry or eat a fairy.

Ella Goodwin (9)
Widey Court Primary School, Crownhill

Clay

On a rainy day
I play with clay
Even though I'm an adult
I like to sculpt
I don't care what they say
Because I have my own way
Of doing things I like
That comes to my mind
I have fun
Singing in the sun
I sing to my favourite song
Will you sing along?

Evie S (9)
Widey Court Primary School, Crownhill

Food

I love food,
Mac 'n' cheese,
Or maybe some baloney, please.
I love chips, they're my fave,
When we have dinner, it's my rave.
The chips, the broccoli, and the carrots,
Begin to get up and boogie with you,
And that is why I love food.

Georgie Sanderson (10)
Widey Court Primary School, Crownhill

Time

Time is slow
When you wait.

Time is fast
When you're late.

Time is short
When you're happy.

Time is big
When you're sad.

Time is everything.

Grace Dalrymple (10)
Widey Court Primary School, Crownhill

Sanrio

S tar Twins sparkle
A nime world
N ew characters excite me
R ainbow colours that brightly shine
I magination runs wild
O ut of this world.

Scarlett Keach (10)
Widey Court Primary School, Crownhill

Extraterrestrial Space Ultimate

I am an alien
No, I am a star
No, I am a superstar
No, I am a mash monster,
No, I am a...
I am an *alien*!

Bailey McClure (10)
Widey Court Primary School, Crownhill

A Carp Journeyed Through Space

"Blop, blop," said the carp in the lake,
But this carp had a different fate.
As the light beamed down on the carp in the lake,
It took it into space.

"Blop, blop," said the carp in the lake
That flew past planes and birds, even Mars,
High into space,
Out with the stars.

"Blob, blob," said the carp that's now in space
"I have a plan," said the silly old carp,
"I'll eat all these boilies up."
He sucked up Saturn, he sucked up Mars,
He sucked on Pluto, he sucked up stars.

"Blob, blob," said the carp, "It's just too hard.
There are too many boilies to eat,
But I have started my daily feast."
As he flew down past planes and birds,
He realised they were planets.

Oh, you silly old carp.

Jamie-Leigh Deverill (10)
Willow Bank Primary School, Thamesmead

Nature's Nocturnal Symphony

The moon ascends, a silver crest,
To light the sky where shadows rest,
The forest hums
A soft midnight song
The stars, like diamonds, glint and glow,
A sparkling dance, a cosmic show,
The brook beneath reflects their gleam,
Its waters wearing night's own dream,
A breeze flows through with cool caress,
Whispering secrets none confess,
The willows bow, their branches low,
As whispers through their leaves do flow,
The wolves let loose a howling call,
Their echoes rise, then slowly fall,
The night responds calm, serene,
Each cricket plays its violin,
A concert where the stars begin,
The night in gold so pure,
All melodies will endure,
Through nature's night,
A world takes flight,

Where shadows live and stars light a realm of wonder, calm and grace,
A sacred, timeless, boundless space.

Tianna Hamilton-Walker (10)
Willow Bank Primary School, Thamesmead

The Beauty Of The Starlight

Up above,
Where starlight softly glows,
A canvas of dreams,
And endless themes,
The sky is a blanket woven,
With threads of blue,
A celestial dance,
Old and true.

In twilight's hush,
Where shadows fall,
A million whispers echo,
One laugh,
One of all.
The whispers of the past,
And those left to be,
In harmony a symphony,
Of destiny.

So let us lift our eyes,
And gaze at the sky,
And let our spirits stir,
As wind whistles by.

For up there,
Where the sky meets the Earth below,
Like a beauty only curiosity can show.

So next time you look,
At the stars in the night,
Look at the beauty,
Of the starlight.

Zainab Balougun (10)
Willow Bank Primary School, Thamesmead

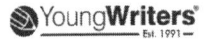

Christmas

It's that time of the year again, Christmastime
Kids playing happily under the cold night sky
It's that time of the year again, Christmastime
Frosty and windy, cold and snowy
The cold breeze passes through the foggy sky
It's that time of the year again, Christmastime
Hanging up your decorations with such joy and divine
It's that time of the year again, Christmastime
Kids opening presents, happy or sad or angry or mad
It's that time of the year again, Christmastime
Santa delivering presents in the dark night sky
It's that time of the year again, Christmastime
The fire crackles, warm and bright
Chasing the shadows through the night
It's that time of the year again.

Aseda Asare (10)
Willow Bank Primary School, Thamesmead

The Assassination Of The King

Outside the kingdom, the assassin awaits. At night, he plots a crime to assassinate. The assassin disappears in a flash and the next thing you know, he's in front of the castle door.
"There he is..." he grins under his mask.
The king is sitting on his throne, ordering people with his loud tone.
At night it is time, the assassin sneaks into the castle like a ninja. He is about to stab the king until *bang!* A loud sound in the distance frightens the assassin. But wait, there is blood around the room.
"I'm killing the king, not you..."

Tobi Adetula (11)
Willow Bank Primary School, Thamesmead

Creative Cultures

Japan's jazzy jive jammed the streets, sharing their jubilant and joyful energy around the town.
China's cheerful cha-cha, with dragons ever so delicate and delightful patterns with such beautiful dynamics.
Ireland's immaculate instruments play through the whole village, with plaited dark indigo skirts.
Spain's spectacular, special sculpture, the fountain of Neptune, monuments, and they're delicious!
Georgia's glamorous khachapuri, which tastes so unique, the traditional glamour of the world.
Such creative cultures!

Love Nwadikeduruibe (11)
Willow Bank Primary School, Thamesmead

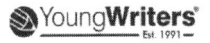

Summer Dreams

As you soar through the sky,
Full of excitement,
Each waterslide screaming your name.
Finding it impossible to contain,
The pain in your legs quickly vanishes,
As you get to your favourite place,
The beach.
The soft, slippery sand and
The strong waves crashing onto land.
The sun above the air so sweet.
I find a spot where skies and waters meet.
The horizon.

Kaydie Green Mengot (10)
Willow Bank Primary School, Thamesmead

Beyond The Mystical Sea

Beyond the sea, so blue and deep
Is where the ocean's finest creatures hunt and creep.
Beyond the sea, so far away
Lies a coral reef underneath the waves.

Beyond the sea, a land of mysteries
Is where dreams take flight and spirits roam free.
Beyond the sea, we'll find our key
Because there's a life with fantasy,
Waiting for you and me.

Christabel Jaiyesimi (11)
Willow Bank Primary School, Thamesmead

Emotions

Happy, sad, angry and scared too.
There's a lot of emotions inside of you.
Worry, anxiety, embarrassment, envy and boredom too,
You can control by thinking what's inside of you.

You're your own person and no matter what you feel,
You are special in your own way.
So what do you say? Hip, hip, hooray!

Jayden Mclellen (11)
Willow Bank Primary School, Thamesmead

Cats

I had a cat
Who acted like a bat,
And chased cheeky rats,
The cat likes to prowl
Around the house it will growl
It scratches the mat
And demands its food
In such a good mood
I jump to the moon.
The cat meows
And says goodbye
As it scratches the wood
Beside my thigh.
I love my cat.

Maris Obi (11)
Willow Bank Primary School, Thamesmead

Dragons

D azzling dragons soaring through the sky
R ed flaming eyes that could make you cry
A ncient legends with scary scales
G liding in the stormy gales
O versized wings and sharp claws
N ot forgetting their dangerous jaws
S creaming out their mighty roars.

Ethan Turrell (10)
Willow Bank Primary School, Thamesmead

The Mystical River

Glistening waters, a mystical flow,
Glowing brightly in the dark below.
A river of dreams,
Where the stars gleam.
Making you shiver,
In the gloomiest of whispers.
In the dead of the night,
The beauty reveals,
Splish and *splash* is all you can hear!

Inaaya Mozaddid (10)
Willow Bank Primary School, Thamesmead

The Solar System Sequence

The solar system sequence is very, very frequent.
In the middle is the sun. Is it just there for fun?
No, it's the light of the world, shared among all the planets.
The solar system being lined up is very rare,
But if you want to find out more, go out to space if you dare!

Jesunifemi Ogunkoya (10)
Willow Bank Primary School, Thamesmead

Spring

S pring blossoms when new life begins
P eaches and apples grow on fresh trees
R ain so gentle you can't feel a thing
I can't resist the smell of spring
N either will you
G roups of animals get together to celebrate spring!

Azizah Balogun (8)
Willow Bank Primary School, Thamesmead

Winter Is Here!

W hite Christmases are the best
I cy cold temperatures are such a pest.
N o green to be seen anywhere
T rees with no leaves sway in the breeze.
E veryone is having lots of fun
R eindeer are pulling Santa's sleigh.

Ruby Vuong (9)
Willow Bank Primary School, Thamesmead

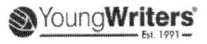

Beyond The Stars

Beneath the stars, so far, so wide
Galaxies spin in endless grace
A cosmic dance in infinite space
Neptune glows, with colours bright
A canvas painted in the night
Through blackened voids and distant light
We sail through the night.

Millie Ross (10)
Willow Bank Primary School, Thamesmead

Learn

L isten closely, open your mind
E xplore new things, there's so much more to find
A sk lots of questions; don't be shy
R ead and write, let your thoughts fly
N ever stop learning, and reach for the sky!

Veron Selmani (10)
Willow Bank Primary School, Thamesmead

The Mighty Ogiso

The mighty Ogiso
On a throne with the phone.
Watch him roar at a drawer.
The mighty Ogiso
Fierce like a lion
Everyone surrendering
He is the greatest of them all.
Mighty Ogiso
The king of Benin.

Demi Adeson (10)
Willow Bank Primary School, Thamesmead

Culture

Culture, culture
As we know, people are being bullied every single day
Race or background, it doesn't really matter
Because we are all the same
We should all love, respect and value each other's culture.

Godsglory Medayese (9)
Willow Bank Primary School, Thamesmead

Our Bunny

Our bunny cost us a lot of money
We named the bunny Honey
Honey is funny
He has a friend named Runny
It is very sunny
Runny has a baby brother named Tunny
They are all happy and lucky.

Zino Ubu (10)
Willow Bank Primary School, Thamesmead

YOUNG WRITERS INFORMATION

We hope you have enjoyed reading this book – and that you will continue to in the coming years.

If you're the parent or family member of an enthusiastic poet or story writer, do visit our website **www.youngwriters.co.uk/subscribe** and sign up to receive news, competitions, writing challenges and tips, activities and much, much more! There's lots to keep budding writers motivated!

If you would like to order further copies of this book, or any of our other titles, then please give us a call or order via your online account.

Young Writers
Remus House
Coltsfoot Drive
Peterborough
PE2 9BF
(01733) 890066
info@youngwriters.co.uk

Join in the conversation!
Tips, news, giveaways and much more!

YoungWritersUK   YoungWritersCW
youngwriterscw   youngwriterscw

Scan Me!